Letters from the Rock

1 & 2 Peter

Loren VanGalder

Spiritual Father Publications

All scripture quotations, unless otherwise indicated, are taken from the Holy Bible, New International Version®, NIV®. Copyright ©1973, 1978, 1984, 2011 by Biblica, Inc.™All rights reserved worldwide. The "NIV" and "New International Version" are trademarks registered in the United States Patent and Trademark Office by Biblica, Inc.™

Scripture quotations marked Amplified (AMP) are from the Amplified New Testament. Copyright ©1954, 1958, 1987 by the Lockman Foundation. Used by Permission of Zondervan Publishing House. All rights reserved.

Scripture quotations marked Good News Translation (GNT) are from the Good News Translation. Copyright © 1992 by American Bible Society.

Scripture quotations marked NASB are from the New American Standard Bible, Copyright © 1960, 1962, 1963, 1968, 1971, 1972, 1973, 1975, 1977, 1995 by The Lockman Foundation.

Quotations marked New Living Translation (NLT) are from the Holy Bible, New Living Translation, copyright © 1996. Used by permission of Tyndale House Publishers, Inc., Wheaton, Illinois 60189. All rights reserved.

Scripture quotations marked (PHILLIPS) are from The New Testament in Modern English by J.B Phillips copyright © 1960, 1972 J. B. Phillips. Administered by The Archbishops' Council of the Church of England. Used by Permission.

Copyright © 2019 by Loren VanGalder. All rights reserved.

ISBN-13: 978-1-7336556-5-1

Contents

Introduction Grace and peace in abundance)1 Peter 1:1-2)...1

1 One of many reasons to praise God   (1 Peter 1:3-5)...7

2 How to survive and thrive amid trials
(1 Peter 1:6-25)...13

3 A holy priesthood   (1 Peter 2:1-10)...21

4 The life of a pilgrim and exile   (1 Peter 2:11-25)...27

5 Relationships   (1 Peter 3:1-12)...35

6 Extreme submission   (1 Peter 3:13-22)...45

7 A new perspective on suffering   (1 Peter 4)...53

8 Counsel for elders, youth, and everyone (1 Peter 5)...67

2 Peter...75

9 How to never fall   (2 Peter 1:1-11)...77

10 Peter's experience   (2 Peter 1:12-21)...87

11 False teachers and their destruction   (2 Peter 2)...91

12 Christ is coming soon   (2 Peter 3)...103

Introduction

Grace and peace in abundance
1 Peter 1:1-3

¹ Peter, an apostle of Jesus Christ,

To God's elect, exiles scattered throughout the provinces of Pontus, Galatia, Cappadocia, Asia and Bithynia, ² who have been chosen according to the foreknowledge of God the Father, through the sanctifying work of the Spirit, to be obedient to Jesus Christ and sprinkled with his blood:

Grace and peace be yours in abundance.

The author doesn't need to introduce himself; every believer knew that Jesus had a special relationship with this disciple. He is now a leader among the apostles, who are Christ's representatives sent with his authority. Peter wrote this letter between AD 62 and 64, possibly from Rome, during Emperor Nero's persecution, in which Christians were tortured and killed. Peter himself would be crucified upside down during this persecution.

The recipients
Three words describe the believers who received this letter:

- **Elect.** Peter immediately steps into a controversy that has not been resolved in two thousand years: Free will versus God's sovereign election. We can't avoid or deny the many times the Bible says that God chose us. There are various ways of understanding it. One possibility is that God knows the future (he operates outside our concept of space and time), giving him prior knowledge of who would accept him and who would not. We won't resolve the debate here, but being chosen provides security and status in the eyes of God. He knows you and wants you to be part of his family. Most of Peter's readers were Jews, who already had a very clear concept of Abraham's election and Israel as God's chosen people. Now this election extends to those who trust in Christ.

- **Exiles.** We are pilgrims and foreigners in this world, expatriates, living outside our native land. With so much movement and so many refugees in today's world, it is common to experience being an expat (I'm an expatriate American living in Costa Rica).

- **Scattered.** The dispersion of believers began with Steven's death, recorded in Acts 7 and 8. God indeed promised the land of Canaan to Abraham and his descendants, but he also wants his people to be salt and light in the world. Whether we are sent as missionaries or scattered by persecution, God allows this dispersion to enable the spread of the Gospel. The famous "pax romana" facilitated travel in a large part of the world.

The only sure thing for them (aside from a measure of security as part of the Roman Empire) was their relationship with God, which is worth a lot! We live with that tension of being different, even in our native land. As Christians, we are a minority, and we are subject to a world system that is under the dominion of the evil one.

All these churches are located in what is now Turkey, an area primarily evangelized by Paul, the apostle to the Gentiles. He planted the church in Galatia, but the Holy Spirit didn't allow him to go to Bithynia or Asia (Acts 16:6-7).

They were changed. How?
We see the trinity (Father, Son, and Holy Spirit) in verse 2:

- The Father chose us for salvation.
- Jesus paid the price of our salvation on the cross.
- The sanctifying work of the Holy Spirit changes us.

The NLT says, "His *Spirit has made you holy.*" You are a saint! Not in the sense that we are exceptionally spiritual or miracle workers (as in the Catholic Church), but because we have been taken out of the world to form a new community, cleansed by Jesus' blood. From the beginning, when God first calls us and starts to make us hunger and thirst for a living relationship with him, the Holy Spirit works in us to bring us to salvation, guide us, and keep us safe in a hostile world. His sanctifying work is a continual, lifelong process to conform us to Christ's image. The Spirit convicts us of sin, teaches us how to live, and gives us the power to resist temptation and overcome sin.

The purpose of our election

The Bible gives various purposes for our salvation, but Peter has two in mind as he starts this letter:

- **Obedience to Jesus Christ.** Serving him as Lord of everything. That was a hard lesson for a strong-willed man like Peter, but he could testify that it was worth it.

- **Redemption by Jesus' blood.** Christ paid the price for our sin and rebellion, and bought us from our slavery to the devil and fleshly desires, restoring our relationship to God and cleansing us from all sin.

How do these two fit into your understanding of being a Christian? Are you grateful for Jesus' sacrifice, which paid for your redemption? Is obeying Jesus a serious goal in your life? What Peter doesn't name (an abundant life, happiness, prosperity, a blessed family, or personal peace) shows how commonly we misunderstand what is important in the Christian life.

The blessing

That's just the greeting! Now Peter blesses us, the usual start to a letter, with words similar to Paul's blessings in his letters: grace and peace.

- **Grace.** God's unmerited favor. In a challenging situation, it is comforting to know that the Christian life does not depend on your efforts and good works, but on God's grace. He chooses to love you and pour out his favor and blessings on you. It's freeing to rest in that grace and let God work through the Holy Spirit.

- **Peace.** In a world full of conflicts and inner struggles, God's supernatural peace sustains us during the storms. First, peace with God, then inner peace, and finally peace with others, including our enemies.

Peter's prayer is that this peace and grace would overflow in us and be multiplied. Is that your experience? Or are you grateful for just a few moments of peace in a church service? God wants to multiply his grace and peace in you, filling all of your life.

1

One of many reasons to praise God
1 Peter 1:3-5

³ Praise be to the God and Father of our Lord Jesus Christ! In his great mercy he has given us new birth into a living hope through the resurrection of Jesus Christ from the dead, ⁴ and into an inheritance that can never perish, spoil or fade. This inheritance is kept in heaven for you, ⁵ who through faith are shielded by God's power until the coming of the salvation that is ready to be revealed in the last time.

It is easy to quickly read through these three verses and miss the rich content. To avoid that, we will follow the progression of thought with a series of questions and answers (*everything in italics is taken from various translations of the Bible*).

Praise be to the God and Father of our Lord Jesus Christ! Let us give thanks to the God and Father of our Lord Jesus Christ!

Of course, God is worthy of all the praise, but it is more than singing some worship songs; we want to worship in truth, understanding the reason for our worship.

So why do we praise him?
We have been born again. A baby doesn't choose to be born; it is totally out of their control. As we saw in verse 2, God chose us and did the saving work. Jesus said we have to become like little children to enter the kingdom (Matthew 18:3), and God made that possible by this new birth, which is the only way to enter the kingdom (John 3:3). Here, and in verse 23 of the same chapter,

are the only times aside from John 3 that the Bible uses the words "born again," although various times it speaks of a spiritual birth. The good news is that we can start over, with everything made new, like a newborn baby (2 Corinthians 5:17).

How could God do something we are so undeserving of?

By His boundless mercy. Mercy is "compassion or forgiveness shown toward someone whom it is within one's power to punish or harm." God is rich in mercy and gives the believer this same ability to feel compassion, empathy, and love for people, especially those who are suffering. Jesus said: *"Blessed are the merciful, for they will be shown mercy"* (Matthew 5:7).

How do we come to experience this salvation?

Through the resurrection of Jesus Christ from the dead. To allow us into his kingdom and restore our relationship with him, a sacrifice was necessary. Since God is perfectly righteous, someone had to pay for our offenses, our sins. The only effective sacrifice had to be perfect, and only God is perfect. It started with Jesus' death on the cross, but without the resurrection, there would be no victory or hope. Jesus' resurrection guarantees eternal life and victory over sin and death.

What benefit do we receive? What is God's purpose for us?

1. *A life full of hope, a living hope. Now we live with great expectation.* Many of us had no hope. We were disappointed and disillusioned with the empty promises the world offered us in terms of money and pleasure. Christ's resurrection assures us that there is hope; the one who conquered death can overcome any problem in our daily lives. To live without hope is a living hell; a living

hope enables us to endure suffering. God wants to give you a new hope, so you can live each day with great expectation of what God is going to do.

2. *An inheritance that can never perish, spoil, or fade. We have a priceless inheritance—an inheritance that is kept in heaven for you, pure and undefiled, beyond the reach of change and decay.* We not only receive forgiveness of sins and a "mansion" in heaven, but also an inheritance. When was the last time you thought about the inheritance God has for you? The Jews' promised inheritance was the land of Canaan, but for the Christian, a child of the King, Jesus said it is *"the kingdom prepared for you since the creation of the world"* (Matt. 25:34).

What is that inheritance like?

I have known people who were counting on a great inheritance from their parents, but then a house burned down, the stock market crashed, the antiques got damaged, or there was a family fight, and they got nothing. There is no guarantee of an inheritance in this world, but your inheritance as God's child is:

1. Indestructible, incorruptible. It is not of this world; it is not material.
2. Pure. Nothing and nobody can contaminate it. It is beautiful in its purity.
3. Undefiled. It cannot spoil or fade. It will not change with time. It is eternal.
4. Reserved in heaven for you. It has your name on it.
5. Guaranteed. It is so vital that God guarantees it with his Spirit: *When you believed, you were marked in him with a seal, the promised Holy Spirit, who is a deposit guaranteeing our inheritance until the redemption of*

those who are God's possession—to the praise of his glory (Ephesians 1:13-14).

Paul spoke about the dynamic of our inheritance, as God's adopted children, in Galatians 4:1-7:

What I am saying is that as long as an heir is underage, he is no different from a slave, although he owns the whole estate. The heir is subject to guardians and trustees until the time set by his father. So also, when we were underage, we were in slavery under the elemental spiritual forces of the world. But when the set time had fully come, God sent his Son, born of a woman, born under the law, to redeem those under the law, that we might receive adoption to sonship. Because you are his sons, God sent the Spirit of his Son into our hearts, the Spirit who calls out, "Abba, Father." So you are no longer a slave, but God's child; and since you are his child, God has made you also an heir.

Who receives these blessings?

1. *You.* Every believer, although not everyone will make it to heaven to claim their inheritance.

Some enemies attack us to destroy us and steal our inheritance, but God has a provision for that threat as well:

2. *Those shielded by God's power.* Without that protection, it is very possible to fall and lose everything. There is no question that God has the power to protect us, but here we get to our part, and that can be dicey...

How do you appropriate that protection?

Through faith. The entire Christian life is by faith. We have already seen that God does great things for us, and we will see many more in this letter, but we have to keep the faith. Doubts will afflict us and our faith will be attacked on every side, but we must stand firm in our faith in God and his Word.

How long?
Until the coming of our salvation. We are already saved, but we haven't experienced the fullness of that salvation, the manifestation of everything our faith means.

When will we receive the fullness of our salvation?
It is ready to be revealed in the last time. For most of us, that means after death. When Christ comes to establish his kingdom, we will receive our inheritance, the redemption of our bodies, and the reward God has prepared for us.

This is good news! In all of life's tribulations, we need to focus on the great work God has done for us, because sometimes it can seem like a dream.

2

How to survive and thrive amid trials
1 Peter 1:6-25

Sometimes you may read God's Word and see all the blessings he promises us, but you can't identify with them. You might doubt your salvation, or think you missed out on it because of your sin. The believers who received this letter had suffered greatly and lived with that tension.

Suffering in all kinds of trials
⁶ In all this you greatly rejoice, though now for a little while you may have had to suffer grief in all kinds of trials.

Reflecting on the blessings in the first part of this chapter, do you rejoice because of all God has done for you? It says you have suffered *"for a little while."* It could be that they accepted Christ and never had that problem-free "honeymoon." Instead, it had been nonstop persecution and *"all kinds of trials."* Thank God that they are only temporary. God may allow them, but he can also rescue us from them.

Why were they being persecuted?

- They refused to worship the emperor as a god.
- They wouldn't worship in the pagan temples, depriving the temple businesses of significant revenue.
- They rejected the immorality of pagan culture.

Do you feel like your trials will never end? Are you suffering grief in all kinds of trials right now? Fill your thoughts with the glorious things God has prepared for you, and you can rejoice during the trials.

Refined in the fire
⁷ These have come so that the proven genuineness of your faith—of greater worth than gold, which perishes even though refined by fire—may result in praise, glory and honor when Jesus Christ is revealed.

What a glorious day it will be when Jesus is revealed! All these trials will seem like nothing, as your faith passes the test and is proved genuine, resulting in praise, glory and honor. Do you receive honor because you made it through? Or does Jesus get the glory because he helped you make it? Probably both!

In this life, we are refined, like gold. You may be in the fire right now, but God knows what he's doing. These trials reveal whether your faith (which is more precious than gold) is genuine. It's better to have it tested now than to find out it's not genuine when Christ comes. God uses the trials for your benefit, because *we know that in all things God works for the good of those who love him, who have been called according to his purpose* (Romans 8:28). Trials build patience and perseverance in us (Rom. 5:3, 4; James 1:2, 3).

Where are you in this process of your faith being refined? Are you in the fire? What is the fire revealing about you and your faith?

Indescribable joy
⁸ Though you have not seen him, you love him; and even though you do not see him now, you believe in him and are filled with an inexpressible and glorious joy, ⁹ for you are receiving the result of your faith, the salvation of your souls.

You are saved the moment you accept Jesus, but the process of sanctification starts at that point. You are somewhere in that process now; a big part of it is holding onto your faith, growing in it, and having that faith tested. You will experience more and more of the riches of salvation as you grow in your relationship with Christ, which fills you with an inexpressible and glorious joy. That is the object of your faith, not prosperity or happiness.

We walk by faith, not by sight. Peter is a faithful witness of Christ; he had seen Jesus and walked with him, but we don't have to see him to love him. Loving him without seeing him is true faith, which is strengthened by trials and results in intimacy and joy in your relationship with him. Love, faith, and joy characterize the Christian life.

More privileged than prophets and angels

[10] Concerning this salvation, the prophets, who spoke of the grace that was to come to you, searched intently and with the greatest care, [11] trying to find out the time and circumstances to which the Spirit of Christ in them was pointing when he predicted the sufferings of the Messiah and the glories that would follow. [12] It was revealed to them that they were not serving themselves but you, when they spoke of the things that have now been told you by those who have preached the gospel to you by the Holy Spirit sent from heaven. Even angels long to look into these things.

Old Testament prophets received visions and revelations, but they also diligently studied God's Word. Through the Holy Spirit, they had already seen something of the Messiah's suffering and glory, and wanted more details: When would it happen, and under what circumstances? They spoke only in part, but now the Spirit inspires the apostles and other servants of the Lord to declare God's plan and the fulfillment of Old Testament prophecies. Those faithful prophets longed to experience what we take for granted! But God told them that the messages they had received were not for them, but for us. That was hard for those faithful prophets! Even the angels long to look into these things! There are treasures for us in the study of Old Testament prophets.

How should you respond to these wonders?

These aren't just nice doctrines or something we intellectually agree with. This reality of the new birth and God's work in you should revolutionize your daily life. God has done his work; now, despite the trials and suffering, you must respond in faith and do your part:

¹³ Therefore, with minds that are alert and fully sober, set your hope on the grace to be brought to you when Jesus Christ is revealed at his coming.

Here are three things to do as you face trials and temptations:

1. **Brace yourselves, have your minds ready for action.** The Spanish NIV says, "act intelligently." Does that mean that sometimes we act foolishly? I think so. We get lazy and make poor decisions. Peter is calling you to action, but with a mind that is sensitive to God's leading, thinking clearly, and using all your God-given facilities to navigate through the trials. Sometimes it is tempting to stop and get paralyzed, but you have to decide to overcome the fear and uncertainty, carefully reflect on what the Bible says and what you have learned about the Christian life, and act.

2. **Be fully sober and self-controlled, as men who know what they are doing.** In the past, we often acted impulsively. We didn't use good judgment. In these last days, in a secular world that doesn't recognize the

authority of God and his Word (or amid persecution), there's no time for foolish decisions. You can still enjoy life, the abundant life God offers, and not "la vida loca."

3. **Fix your hope on the grace Jesus will bring you.** In these circumstances, you can't set your hopes on success, wealth, material things, or people in this world. All of them will disappoint you. Jesus is your only hope, but Peter knows it can often seem like a dream. To be "hope," it has to be something we are waiting for, which is not part of our current experience. We will only fully experience God's grace when Jesus comes back. That is the hope that enables us to endure the trials now.

Obedient and holy children

¹⁴ As obedient children, do not conform to the evil desires you had when you lived in ignorance. ¹⁵ But just as he who called you is holy, so be holy in all you do; ¹⁶ for it is written: "Be holy, because I am holy."

Many think of Christianity as very rigid, enslaving us with countless rules. Unbelievers believe they are free to live as they want, but Christ said that the one who sins is a slave to sin (Jn. 8:34). The truth is that everyone is shaped by something; in many cases it is the media, the culture, friends, or (as Peter says here) our evil desires. All that has to change when our eyes are opened and we see the results of that life. The truth is that people in the world live in ignorance; we all lived that way. Can you recognize the "evil desires" of your sinful nature and the evil desires that the world encourages you to satisfy? Do they still shape you?

Paul wrote about this in Romans 12:1-2:

Therefore, I urge you, brothers and sisters, in view of God's mercy, to offer your bodies as a living sacrifice, holy and pleasing to

God—this is your true and proper worship. Do not conform to the pattern of this world, but be transformed by the renewing of your mind. Then you will be able to test and approve what God's will is—his good, pleasing and perfect will.

The new life begins by offering our bodies as living sacrifices to God and renewing our minds with God's Word. We recognize the world's pattern and mold, and choose to go a different way, molded by God's Word and Spirit. Only then will you be able to know what is God's will for you; it is good, pleasing, and perfect, contrary to what many in the world think it is.

The standard is high: be holy, just as God is holy; not only in church, but in everything that you do. We are saints, and that identity should impact all aspects of our lives, causing us to live like saints. Jesus is our model and example of a holy life.

A coming judgment

If the desire to please God and experience his perfect plan isn't enough motivation, Peter reminds us of a coming judgment:

[17] Since you call on a Father who judges each person's work impartially, live out your time as foreigners here in reverent fear.

Peter has already spoken of various ways we differ from the world; now he says that we are foreigners, or pilgrims. Do you know what it is to have a reverent fear of God? If you do right, you have nothing to be afraid of. Judgment day will reveal your good works, and you will receive a crown. We have an intimate relationship with God; he is our Father. But there is no exception for persons with God; you may be his son, but he judges everyone impartially. If you have accepted Christ as Lord and Savior, you can be sure of your salvation, but the Father is going to judge your works. How will that judgment go for you?

Jesus' precious blood

¹⁸ For you know that it was not with perishable things such as silver or gold that you were redeemed from the empty way of life handed down to you from your ancestors, ¹⁹ but with the precious blood of Christ, a lamb without blemish or defect. ²⁰ He was chosen before the creation of the world, but was revealed in these last times for your sake.²¹ Through him you believe in God, who raised him from the dead and glorified him, and so your faith and hope are in God.

The source of your confidence is Christ; he paid the price for your redemption with his own blood. God chose him before the creation of the world to be that perfect lamb, to die on the cross as a sacrifice for your sins.

You lived an empty life (other translations say *'futile,' 'worthless,' or 'absurd'*), but it's not your fault—you inherited it from your ancestors. Your family may not understand why you have to reject that way of life, but now you can see how empty it was. Jesus rescued you from it; now all your hope is in him.

Love one another deeply

²² Now that you have purified yourselves by obeying the truth so that you have sincere love for each other, love one another deeply, from the heart.

Peter has presented a clear contrast between the old life in the world and the new life in Christ. It is so radical that the only way to get in is to be born again. When you hear the truth of the Gospel and obey it, God purifies you and fills you with a sincere love. The love you knew in the past was often self-centered and focused on what it could do for you; the love God gives us should impact all of life. God commands us to love deeply, from the heart, and enables us to do so.

Part of God's family

Several times in this first chapter, we have seen references to family:

- Love for our many brothers and sisters (22).
- God as our Father (3 & 17).
- Being born again into his family (3 & 23).
- We are his obedient children (14).

^{23} For you have been born again, not of perishable seed, but of imperishable, through the living and enduring word of God. ^{24} For,

*"All people are like grass,
  and all their glory is like the flowers of the field;
the grass withers and the flowers fall,
^{25} but the word of the Lord endures forever."*

And this is the word that was preached to you.

God's Word endures forever

Peter quotes Isaiah 40:6-8, which compares us with the fragility of grass and flowers. The Word of God is living and active. Only his Word (and our souls) are eternal. That word is the seed, and you have the great privilege of sowing and announcing that word. It is imperishable seed. Are you spreading it? Does the Word of God have the place it deserves in your daily life?

Without a new birth, it is impossible to escape the crazy, empty life of the past. Have you been born again? Where are you in this process of sanctification?

3

A holy priesthood
1 Peter 2:1-10

God did a greater miracle than raising the dead, healing cancer, or casting out a demon: He paid the price for your sin, adopted you as his child, and gave you an inheritance in his kingdom. Mission accomplished. Now, what do you have to do in response to this miracle?

Get rid of some things

¹Therefore, rid yourselves of all malice and all deceit, hypocrisy, envy, and slander of every kind.

First, Peter names five things from your past that have no place in this new life. Are any of them still a problem for you?

- Malice (wickedness, depravity, malignity)
- Deceit (lying)
- Hypocrisy (insincerity, pretense)
- Envy (jealousy, grudges)
- Slander (unkind speech, insulting language)

What would you add that you need to get rid of?

This is the negative part, washing you and allowing God's Word to fall on fertile ground and grow. What is interesting is that this list doesn't include common sins like smoking, drinking, or immoral sex. We may not give much weight to jealousy or unkind speech, but they are important to God.

Many people are used to thinking of Christianity as an endless list of things you can't do, but imposing a set of rules on us is the farthest thing from Peter's mind. In light of our forgiveness, adoption, and inheritance, these things of the sinful nature no longer attract us. What a relief and joy to get rid of things that only destroy us and our families!

Get ready to grow

² Like newborn babies, crave pure spiritual milk, so that by it you may grow up in your salvation, ³ now that you have tasted that the Lord is good.

If you have experienced something of God's goodness and tasted his salvation, you know how good it is, and you want more. We all start as newborn babes, new creatures, when we accept Christ, but we have to grow. How sad to see someone that God saved ten or twenty years ago who hasn't grown up and is still in diapers!

Peter says that it is the pure milk of the Word that produces growth. Just as a baby seeks his mother's breast and milk, so we should desire and seek the Word. The NLT says we should *"cry out for this nourishment."* The nature of God's Word is that the more you get, the more you want. It's addictive! What part does the Word have in your life? Do you eagerly desire that milk? Without it, a baby dies. How has it helped you grow in your salvation in the past? Are you receiving daily nourishment in the Word? It's tragic how many Christians barely open their Bibles.

Living stones in a spiritual house

⁴ As you come to him, the living Stone—rejected by humans but chosen by God and precious to him— ⁵ you also, like living stones, are being built into a spiritual house to be a holy priesthood, offering spiritual sacrifices acceptable to God through Jesus Christ.

How sad, and how it hurts the Father, that his precious son was rejected by his own people. Praise God, you have accepted him and entered into a personal relationship with Christ; now you need to get close to him. Peter calls him a living stone, but then says something radical: We too are living stones. Salvation is not just individual; an integral part of salvation is being part of a spiritual house. God places you as a stone in the wall of that house, where you relate with the other living stones. Buildings are not alive and are not that important to God. We invest enormous amounts of time, energy, and money in our buildings; God is interested in the spiritual house.

In the Greek, it is a command: **Be built as a spiritual house and holy priesthood**. It is not optional, but rather for all Christians, regardless of their level of spirituality or involvement in the church. A single stone (like a single member of our body) is useless without other stones. Is your stone part of a spiritual house? Are you experiencing a rich fellowship with the other stones? Is it a house that glorifies God?

Acceptable sacrifices to God

In the Old Testament, the priests offered the sacrifices. Peter makes a connection with the Old Covenant, but it has undergone significant transformation; notable changes have occurred in how we worship God. We no longer sacrifice sheep and other animals, but God still requires sacrifices, and priests still offer them, except that now we are all priests; we are part of a royal priesthood. That is a great privilege and responsibility. Paul talks about us as living sacrifices (Rom. 12:1); here, Peter talks about spiritual sacrifices, which have to be acceptable to God. Many people make sacrifices to gain others' approval or think they can obligate God to do something. But sacrifices made with an impure or sinful heart, or with the wrong motives, are not acceptable to God. The Old Testament speaks extensively of God rejecting the sacrifices required by the law because his people were in sin. The extreme sacrifice was the sacrifice of Jesus Christ on the cross. God is most pleased by the sacrifice of ourselves; laying down our lives for our brothers and sisters or our families, sacrificing our comfort and time, and denying ourselves for the benefit of others. Everything we do in Jesus' name can be a sacrifice to God: service, worship, and thanksgiving.

Do you see yourself as a priest? God describes a process in which you come to be that priest, as you participate in the church with other living stones and other priests. Offering sacrifices to God is a very high, holy, and privileged calling; it is a place of intimacy with God. How are you doing as a priest? Is there something you can do to be more involved with other living stones?

The cornerstone

⁶ For in Scripture it says:

> *"See, I lay a stone in Zion,*
> *a chosen and precious cornerstone,*
> *and the one who trusts in him*
> *will never be put to shame."*

⁷ Now to you who believe, this stone is precious. But to those who do not believe,

> *"The stone the builders rejected*
> *has become the cornerstone,"*

⁸ and,

> *"A stone that causes people to stumble*
> *and a rock that makes them fall."*

They stumble because they disobey the message—which is also what they were destined for.

Peter quotes Isaiah (8:14 & 28:16) and Psalms (118:22) to confirm the fulfillment of Old Testament prophecies. The church doesn't cancel the Jewish heritage, it completes it. The cornerstone, the foundation stone of this house, is Jesus, placed by the Father as the most important stone in the house. This stone is precious to his Father and to us, but not accepted or valued by the world. They can't understand the importance we give to this stone, and they reject it.

It is interesting that Peter talks so much about stones. Jesus gave him a new name—Peter, which means "rock." His confession of Christ as Lord is the rock on which Christ builds his church.

For the world and other religions, the problem is always Jesus. If we talk about "god" in generic terms, there is no problem, but Jesus is the stone that makes people stumble and the rock that makes them fall. For them, Jesus is a scandal, just as he was for the Jews while he was on this earth. They stumble because of their rebellion; they don't want to obey the Word, and those who disobey it are destined to fall. There is a close connection between unbelief and disobedience, just as faith and obedience are related. An integral part of being a living stone in that spiritual house is a hunger for the Word: feeding on it and obeying it.

Do you trust that stone? The precious promise here is that if you trust in him, you will never be put to shame.

Your identity

[9] But you are a chosen people, a royal priesthood, a holy nation, God's special possession, that you may declare the praises of him who called you out of darkness into his wonderful light. [10] Once you were not a people, but now you are the people of God; once you had not received mercy, but now you have received mercy.

There has been a miraculous transformation: Before, we were not a people, especially we Gentiles. Our rebellion and sin made us God's enemies. We had not received mercy. We were in darkness. We were nothing! But now God has called us to his marvelous light, and in Christ, everything has changed:

- We have received God's mercy.
- We are God's people, his special possession.
- We are a chosen people.
- We are a royal priesthood.
- We are a holy nation.

And what is God's purpose for this great salvation? To declare his works and wonders to the whole world!

As priests, we reflect God's holiness, offer spiritual sacrifices, intercede for others before God, and declare who our God is. Those offerings and sacrifices could be our bodies (Rom. 12:1), money or material things (Philippians 4:18), praise (Hebrews 13:15), or good works (Heb. 13:16).

Throughout the Old Testament, God repeatedly expressed his longing for a people, starting with Abraham, and then the establishment of Israel as a nation. Unfortunately, God was always disappointed, but now, at last, he has his people: you and me.

Look again at who you are, according to God's Word. It is far more important than success, riches, or education. Does this truth shape your identity? Do you have this self-image? Notice again the corporate nature of who we are: A people, a royal priesthood, and a holy nation. It is impossible to experience what God wants for us at home alone, watching a service on TV or the internet.

4

The life of a pilgrim and exile
1 Peter 2:11-25

An exemplary life

11 Dear friends, I urge you, as foreigners and exiles, to abstain from sinful desires, which wage war against your soul. 12 Live such good lives among the pagans that, though they accuse you of doing wrong, they may see your good deeds and glorify God on the day he visits us.

For some reason the NIV translators felt the need to water down the love Peter felt for these believers; the Greek says "beloved." Peter has a father's heart and loves the church, but like any good father, he also has some hard words to share with them. He has just talked about our exalted status (royal priesthood, holy nation). It is tempting for the preacher to focus on those verses and ignore the hard teaching we will see in this portion. The study of an entire biblical book is important if we want to sense God's heart. With this introduction, Peter is preparing us for the "solid food" of these chapters.

We're not home; we live as strangers in a world under the dominion of the evil one. But at the same time, this is the language of warfare, and this war isn't with the world. It is an inner battle for our souls. We are persecuted by unbelievers and attacked by the devil, but our flesh, the old nature with its sinful desires, also battles against the redeemed nature in Christ. We are in a hard place!

The world can't understand this new life. We are foreigners and exiles, pilgrims, and part of a new nation. Our true citizenship is no longer in a country on this earth; we are passing through on the way to our heavenly home. Do you ever feel strange, different, like you don't fit in this world (or even, at times, in your church or your family)? Many have experienced immigrating to another country or living as an expat there. That is what we are in this world: expatriates. If you feel very comfortable here, it may mean that you are wrapped up in the things of this world and are not walking in holiness.

In the world, in the flesh, in the old life before you knew Christ, it is natural to have sinful desires. You may have been satisfying those desires for many years, and still struggle with them. Now you have to reject them and resist that temptation, to maintain your holiness as part of a royal priesthood. It is easier to hide in church and the Christian community, but God calls us to live among unbelievers. As foreigners in a sinful community, we have to be salt and light, and walk in holiness because God is holy.

The world always watches us and expects more of us than of unbelievers. If our lifestyle isn't different, we ruin our testimony, and there is no reason for them to accept Christ. We bring disgrace to Christ's name. They may accuse you of wrongdoing, but don't give them a reason for their criticism. Instead, silence them by your good works.

Unfortunately, there are some Christians who act like saints in church and with their Christian brothers, but at home or on the job, it's another story. They are two-faced, trying to serve two masters, and Christ says that is impossible (Matt. 6:24). Have you ever had that inner struggle? There's no peace. You are miserable as a Christian, without the joy of the Lord, but you can't enjoy the things of the world as you did before. Yes, there still are sinful desires that wage war against your soul. Stay away from them!

Can you say that your conduct among unbelievers is exemplary? Would they have any reason to talk about you and accuse you of wrongdoing? How are your good works? Does your life bring honor and glory to Jesus, so that others can glorify God? Do you know anyone with exemplary conduct who glorifies God through their good works?

Submission to every human authority

13 Submit yourselves for the Lord's sake to every human authority: whether to the emperor, as the supreme authority, 14 or to governors, who are sent by him to punish those who do wrong and to commend those who do right. 15 For it is God's will that by doing good you should silence the ignorant talk of foolish people.

Here, Peter introduces a word that will be important for a good portion of his letter: submission. It is hard for us to submit to God; the sinful nature is rebellious and wants to be in charge, but we must honor authorities here on earth. Although it may be difficult, Christ's love compels us, and through our relationship with him and the new nature he gives us, we can submit. The requirement may seem extreme: To every human authority. Peter gives the example of a king as the supreme authority, and all the governors who serve as his delegated authorities. If a government is working well, those authorities punish wrongdoers and reward those who do right. It seems that the punishment is more common than the commendation, and often without much justice. We should encourage those in authority to do both, recognizing those who have done well.

Again, the goal is to give a good testimony, silencing the ignorance of those who feel that honoring Jesus as King somehow conflicts with our duties as citizens. It would be a new concept for Jews suffering under Roman oppression; there had been rebellions in Judea before and after Christ, eventually resulting in the destruction of Jerusalem and the temple in AD 70.

Every authority includes teachers, bosses, the police, and anyone else who might exercise authority. Who are the authorities in your situation? Can you say that you are subject to them? Or would you have to confess that you have a rebellious attitude? Practicing that submission helps us submit to God and develops humility in us.

Show proper respect to everyone

[16] Live as free people, but do not use your freedom as a cover-up for evil; live as God's slaves. [17] Show proper respect to everyone, love the family of believers, fear God, honor the emperor.

That is the universal guideline we are to follow: Give proper respect and honor to everyone. It is similar to the Golden Rule and expresses our humility as God's servants. We submit voluntarily to God and every human authority. The truth is that we are free, freer than the people in the world, but we can't use that freedom as an excuse to do evil. We must be respectful to everyone, showing them consideration, and esteeming and honoring them. Everyone is made in God's image and is worthy of respect. That respect takes different forms, depending on who the person is:

- For brothers and sisters in Christ (the church, Christ's body): Love (agape love, God's unconditional love).
- For God: Fear, or reverence.
- For the king: Neither love nor fear, but respect for the position he occupies.

Instructions for slaves

18 Slaves, in reverent fear of God submit yourselves to your masters, not only to those who are good and considerate, but also to those who are harsh. 19 For it is commendable if someone bears up under the pain of unjust suffering because they are conscious of God. 20 But how is it to your credit if you receive a beating for doing wrong and endure it? But if you suffer for doing good and you endure it, this is commendable before God.

The first application of this call to submit is for slaves (or servants, those who have a master), of which there were many in the early church. This is a hard word in several ways. First, because Peter doesn't condemn the institution of slavery. He doesn't approve of it, but he accepts it as part of society. The Bible teaches us how to live in the situation we find ourselves in, and to trust God to change it when (or if) he wants to.

When we have to submit, it is easier if the person is good and considerate. However, God calls us to submit to those who are harsh and unbearable, doing so with all respect (without grumbling or speaking ill of the person). Our responsibility is before God; he knows that we are going to suffer unjustly (Christ did), and doesn't promise to free us from it, but instead calls us to endure it patiently. There is nothing special about suffering for wrongdoing, but suffering for doing right is commendable. God sees it, knows about it, and will reward you.

Thank God, there aren't as many slaves today, due in large part to Christian efforts to eliminate slavery. But your job can feel like slavery, and some women feel like their husbands' slaves. You may be suffering for doing right. Are you patiently enduring it? Do you always honor and respect your boss? Can you trust God for relief in his time? God knows what is happening; someday they will be judged, and everything will be set right. God is with you and will take care of you.

Christ's example

²¹ To this you were called, because Christ suffered for you, leaving you an example, that you should follow in his steps.

²² "He committed no sin,
and no deceit was found in his mouth."

²³ When they hurled their insults at him, he did not retaliate; when he suffered, he made no threats. Instead, he entrusted himself to him who judges justly. ²⁴ "He himself bore our sins" in his body on the cross, so that we might die to sins and live for righteousness; "by his wounds you have been healed." ²⁵ For "you were like sheep going astray," but now you have returned to the Shepherd and Overseer of your souls.

What a beautiful ending to this chapter! Peter directs our attention to Christ. If we are tempted to complain about how hard life is and how difficult it is to submit to the authorities, we should reflect on Christ's experience.

Peter says we were called to suffer. Our suffering is nothing compared to the incredible suffering Christ endured on the cross, bearing our sins. If you are suffering, it doesn't necessarily mean you have done something wrong; Christ never sinned or deceived anyone.

In the world, we are told to express our anger. Many Christians try to deny or suppress it because they don't know what to do with the injustice they have suffered. The Christian gives his anger and the situation to the Lord, following Christ's example in suffering:

- Others will insult you: don't retaliate with more insults.

- You will suffer; don't threaten the person responsible for it.
- Give it to God, who judges justly.

You can trust that God will use your suffering for your good. Christ's suffering produced beautiful fruit:

- His death enabled your reconciliation with God. You were a rebellious, lost, and wandering sheep, separated from God by your sin. Jesus paid the price for that sin and restored the relationship with the shepherd of your soul. You are safe once again in his sheep pen.
- He gives you the power to crucify the flesh and die to sin.
- His Holy Spirit gives you the power and motivation to live for righteousness.
- By his stripes you are healed (spiritually and physically, quoting Isaiah 53:5).

Suddenly, your problems and your suffering don't look that big. What a privilege to suffer for doing right, and follow in the footsteps of our Lord and Savior! God looks out for you and takes care of you. Have you returned to the Shepherd and Overseer of your soul?

5

Relationships
1 Peter 3:1-12

Instructions for wives

¹Wives, in the same way submit yourselves to your own husbands so that, if any of them do not believe the word, they may be won over without words by the behavior of their wives, ² when they see the purity and reverence of your lives.

In chapter two we saw the importance of submission in God's kingdom. After the general principle of submission to *"every human institution,"* Peter calls slaves (or servants) to submit, even to a cruel master. Now Peter says that the same applies in a marriage, even with an unbelieving husband. This is a hard word for a woman who may be abused by her husband and feel like a slave! The Bible never expects a woman to endure physical or emotional abuse (she needs to leave that abusive situation for a temporary separation), but neither does it allow for rebellion or divorce in those cases. It is a strong test of obedience to the Word and faith in God. It is not as simple as saying "she has to submit" and blaming her for the suffering. Much compassion and support are required.

The humility shown in submission is a testimony, in this case, to the unsaved husband. A woman's faith and prayer to God are always for his salvation. In every marital problem, the person's eternal salvation and walk with Christ are most important; marriage is only for this world, and when both partners are Spirit-filled, the marriage should significantly improve.

Part of the testimony is what she says, but her godly behavior is even more critical. That principle applies in any situation with unbelievers: our pure and respectful behavior should be our most powerful message. How sad when a Christian's behavior brings shame to the name of Christ.

There may be times when an unsaved husband feels he has lost his wife or is competing with Jesus. She may constantly preach at him and condemn him, to the point that he sees nothing of Christ's love; the same can happen with a Christian husband and an unsaved wife.

Sister, if you are married, how are you doing with your submission, behavior, and respect for your husband? Brother, is your conduct at home and work upright, pure, and respectful?

The beauty of a quiet, gentle spirit

³ Your beauty should not come from outward adornment, such as elaborate hairstyles and the wearing of gold jewelry or fine clothes. ⁴ Rather, it should be that of your inner self, the unfading beauty of a gentle and quiet spirit which is of great worth in God's sight.

Is it a sin to wear jewelry or nice clothes? Is it wrong to look attractive? I don't think so, but modesty should characterize a Christian woman. The problem is elaborate hairstyles, ostentatious jewelry, or immodest or attention-getting clothes. God doesn't look at our appearance; those things don't impress him. Beauty should radiate from inside; God likes a gentle and quiet spirit (AMP: *peaceful spirit, [one that is calm and self-controlled, not overanxious, but serene and spiritually mature]*). That beauty doesn't fade; in fact, it grows more beautiful through the years.

Paul wrote something similar in 1 Timothy 2:9-10: *I also want the women to dress modestly, with decency and propriety, adorning themselves, not with elaborate hairstyles or gold or pearls or expensive clothes, but with good deeds, appropriate for women who profess to worship God.*

Brother, do you honor your wife's desire to cultivate that spirit and not overdo her attention to appearance? Or are you always buying her more jewelry or clothes, urging her to use more makeup, and pushing her to fix her hair? Do you look at other women and their appearance so that your wife feels jealous and insecure? And do you dedicate more time to what is in your heart than to your appearance? It's not unusual for a man to devote as much energy and money to his clothes and appearance as a woman does.

Sister, do you devote excessive money, time, and energy to your hair, jewelry and clothes? Do you have that gentle and quiet spirit? Is there something you need to change?

I know this is a delicate topic, but the way many women (and especially young women) dress in church is a stumbling block to men. Some Christians have reacted against legalistic churches and their ultra-conservative dress, but the Christian woman must remember that her life is a testimony and should honor the Lord. Would you be comfortable in that outfit in Jesus' presence? Brother, you need to guide your wife and daughters in this matter.

Sarah's example

⁵ For this is the way the holy women of the past who put their hope in God used to adorn themselves. They submitted themselves to their own husbands, ⁶ like Sarah, who obeyed Abraham and called him her lord. You are her daughters if you do what is right and do not give way to fear.

Submission and modesty characterized godly women of the past. Sarah is the example for women; she obeyed Abraham and called him her lord. Reading some of the stories of their marriage (Genesis 12:10-20; 16:1-7; 20:1-18), it's obvious that Abraham was not a model husband. Sarah may have been unable to conceive because she suffered so much in their relationship.

This teaching is not popular today. Many Christians believe that a woman's submission to her husband no longer applies in today's world. Even in homes and churches where it is practiced, many times the submission is in name only; it is obvious (and accepted) that the woman is really in charge. That's a shame, because the Bible is very clear that God-given order is always in fashion. We have a lot to learn from these holy women of the past.

God's will for the wife

- **Hope in God.** Like slaves with cruel masters, her hope and faith are in God. There is no perfect man, and submission is not conditional on the husband's behavior.
- **Obey her husband.** Not grumbling, complaining, or kicking and fighting, like the Hebrews on the Exodus, but with her heart. Again, "obedience" sounds inappropriate in today's culture.
- **Call him lord.** A title of great respect, recognizing the position God has given him. Obviously not in the same way that Jesus is her Lord.
- **Do what is right.** Despite the temptation to disobey or seek revenge, always do what is pleasing to God, and be busy serving and doing good deeds.
- **Do not give way to fear.** How interesting that Peter would include this. He probably had seen women abused by and afraid of their husbands. The controlling, abusive man is in sin, and may dominate his wife with that fear.

God wants to free every woman from fear, through her faith in God.

Instructions for husbands

⁷ Husbands, in the same way be considerate as you live with your wives, and treat them with respect as the weaker partner and as heirs with you of the gracious gift of life, so that nothing will hinder your prayers.

When Peter says *"in the same way,"* he is commanding men to have the same attitudes required of slaves toward their masters and of wives toward their husbands. It is true that God has given the husband authority, but there are times when, in love, he must submit to his wife. Christ is our example, and he never lorded it over his disciples nor us today. The husband should demonstrate the same love, respect, and humility that is required of slaves and women.

Peter has less to say to men, but it is very important.

The necessary mindset toward his wife:

- **She is the weaker (more delicate or fragile) partner.** That doesn't mean a woman can't be strong and work. Men are often weaker emotionally. In the past, men were more chivalrous and showed more loving care for their wives, in small ways like opening doors and giving them preference. We need to remember that in some aspects she is more fragile. The husband should help his wife with household tasks and childcare, especially if she is working.
- **She is a co-heir of the gracious gift of life.** She is your sister in Christ, and has gifts and a calling for her life. The man is responsible to encourage her relationship with Christ, taking the initiative to pray, worship, and share

the Bible together. Too often it is the woman who longs for more spirituality in the marriage.

The man's behavior:

- **Always treat her considerately and with understanding.** The Amplified Bible says: "*with great gentleness and tact, and with an intelligent regard for the marriage relationship.*" And J. B. Phillips' paraphrase says: "*you husbands should try to understand the wives you live with*"! Good luck! That may require divine intervention, but it is something we men must work at, to learn God's principles and purposes for marriage, and understand her desires, challenges, and frustrations. Learn her strengths and weaknesses. That means dedicating energy to the relationship and truly getting to know her. Reflect on who she is and what is happening in her life right now. We reap what we sow, and many men are not very considerate or wise in the way they treat their wives and what they sow into their lives. Then they are surprised when she doesn't want physical intimacy or neglects her appearance, the house, or other family responsibilities.

- **Treat her with respect and honor.** After Christ, she is the most precious thing in your life, more important than your kids, your relatives, or your friends. Treat her in such a way that she knows you value what she says and are listening to her. Accept and respect your differences. Men often fail to show much respect for their wives; instead of honoring them, they make fun of them and put them down in front of their friends and families. Treasure and celebrate her femininity, and study her to learn what is most important to her.

The result of ignoring these things and not treating her right is hindered prayers. It is a specific application of what Jesus taught in Matthew 5:23-24; we have to resolve problems with others before we come to worship God. Could this be the reason some of your prayers go unanswered? The marital relationship is of great importance to God. Paul says it is a mystery, similar to the relationship of Christ and the church. The man who mistreats his wife suffers spiritually. When your relationship is right, God opens the windows of heaven.

Other New Testament passages also teach about authority and submission in marriage (1 Cor. 7, Eph. 5:22-33, Colossians 3:18-19). For men, Ephesians 5:25-27 may be the most important command: *Husbands, love your wives, just as Christ loved the church and gave himself up for her to make her holy, cleansing her by the washing with water through the word, and to present her to himself as a radiant church, without stain or wrinkle or any other blemish, but holy and blameless.*

Guidance for every relationship

[8] Finally, all of you, be like-minded, be sympathetic, love one another, be compassionate, and humble. [9] Do not repay evil with evil or insult with insult. On the contrary, repay evil with blessing, because to this you were called so that you may inherit a blessing.

Summarizing this section on submission and relationships, Peter includes counsel that applies to slaves and masters, husbands and wives, and every relationship:

- Be like-minded.
- Be sympathetic with each other.
- Love one another (as brothers and sisters).
- Be compassionate and tenderhearted.
- Be humble.

- Do not repay evil with evil or insult with insult.
- Bless others.

How are you doing with these? God called you to inherit a blessing. Are you experiencing it? Peter quotes Psalm 34:12-16 as a summary of what he has just written:

¹⁰ For,

> "Whoever would love life
> and see good days
> must keep their tongue from evil
> and their lips from deceitful speech.
> ¹¹ They must turn from evil and do good;
> they must seek peace and pursue it.
> ¹² For the eyes of the Lord are on the righteous
> and his ears are attentive to their prayer,
> but the face of the Lord is against those who do evil."

Do you want the Lord's eyes on you? Do you want his ears to be attentive to your prayers? Can you confidently say that they are? What evidence do you have of that?

Do you love life? What are your days like? Happy? Or is life a boring routine or a heavy burden? Are your days long and hard?

Peter has given us an unusual prescription for good relationships with God and others: Submission. His desire, and God's desire for you, is not to load you up with religious obligations, but to set you free to love God and others, have a great family, and enjoy life. Besides that, we need to:

- Keep from speaking evil.
- Keep from deceitful speech or lies.
- Turn from evil.
- Do good.

- Seek peace in every situation; God blesses the peacemaker.
- Pursue peace; do everything you can to keep the peace.

The decision is yours. God's Word is clear, and the promise is sure. It is hard to live with the Lord's face against you. God wants to bless you with happy days, but you have to live life his way.

6

Extreme submission
1 Peter 3:13-22

Peter has shared instructions on how to have a happy life as he concludes the teaching on submission, but a nightmare of persecution and even death has left his readers confused. It's an old dilemma: If God is sovereign, why does he allow the righteous to suffer? Why do I have to submit to a cruel master or husband? Maybe after reading these promises, you too have thought: "I have done all that, and I still don't see the blessing." Peter's solution is not easy, but it is consistent: More submission. Our faith enables us to make an extreme surrender to Christ, and that perspective impacts all of life.

Suffering because of righteousness
¹³ Who is going to harm you if you are eager to do good?

Their answer? "Practically everyone! Sometimes it seems that the closer I get to Jesus, the more I suffer!" And Peter responds, from personal experience: "We live in a cruel world, under the dominion of the evil one. There is no guarantee that he won't hurt you, despite your good nature. Look at what he did to God's Son!" It doesn't make sense to hurt someone who came to save and heal us, or the Christian who wants to bless others, but that is the nature of our fallen world.

¹⁴ But even if you should suffer for what is right, you are blessed. "Do not fear their threats; do not be frightened."

Peter offers us three words of comfort and encouragement:

- **You are blessed.** Maybe Peter was thinking of the Beatitudes: *Blessed are those who are persecuted because of righteousness, for theirs is the kingdom of heaven. Blessed are you when people insult you, persecute you and falsely say all kinds of evil against you because of me. Rejoice and be glad, because great is your reward in heaven, for in the same way they persecuted the prophets who were before you* (Matt. 5:10-12). God knows everything. Trust him for his blessing and reward.
- **Do not fear their threats.** Peter may have been citing Isaiah 8:12, which, in its context, gives us a good perspective of God's will: *[11] This is what the Lord says to me with his strong hand upon me, warning me not to follow the way of this people: [12] "Do not call conspiracy everything this people calls a conspiracy; do not fear what they fear, and do not dread it. [13] The Lord Almighty is the one you are to regard as holy, he is the one you are to fear, he is the one you are to dread. [14] He will be a holy place; for both Israel and Judah he will be stone that causes people to stumble and a rock that makes them fall.* We don't think like the world.
- **Do not be frightened.** It helps to know ahead of time that there will be persecution and opposition in this world; don't be surprised if people don't like you because you are a Christian.

As we trust in God's blessing and are freed from fear, we can choose a radical new response to persecution: Don't resist those who persecute you or defend yourself, but honor Christ and testify about him.

Honor Christ in your heart as Lord

15 But in your hearts revere Christ as Lord. Always be prepared to give an answer to everyone who asks you to give the reason for the hope that you have. But do this with gentleness and respect, 16 keeping a clear conscience, so that those who speak maliciously against your good behavior in Christ may be ashamed of their slander. 17 For it is better, if it is God's will, to suffer for doing good than for doing evil.

First, we have to honor Christ as Lord in our hearts. What does that mean? We are his. As our Lord, he sits on the throne of our hearts and directs our lives, but he also cares for us as his sheep. Christ is our friend, but He is also our Lord, and we always have to honor him. When he governs our thoughts and emotions, nothing the enemy does can move us. Submission to authorities in this world is important, but submission to Christ's lordship enables us to overcome the trials of this life.

Once again, Peter says that suffering is part of life in this world, and may even be God's will for us; it is better to suffer for doing good than for doing evil.

Peter's radical teaching, which is precisely what he learned from his Master, as recorded in Matthew 5:44, is that we are always to love our enemies and pray for them. We don't hide in the safety of the church or avoid the world to protect ourselves from their unwarranted attacks. Part of honoring Christ is being his exemplary ambassador in this world. We want the slanderers to know Christ.

- Amid the persecution, it will be evident that you have a hope that goes beyond a better life in this world, and it will get unbelievers' attention.
- Some will ask about the reason for your hope and how it is possible to be joyful in persecution. The Holy Spirit may

be opening their hearts to Christ. Do you know how to share what Christ has done in your life, what we call your "testimony"?
- You have to be prepared ahead of time so you aren't caught off guard, unable to explain the Gospel or the reason for your hope. Study the Bible and books on apologetics (the reasons for your faith), and, if possible, take classes on evangelism.
- You may not always feel like evangelizing, but the words are unambiguous: "*always*," and "*to everyone.*" Are you available?
- Do it with gentleness, humility, and respect. It may seem strange that Peter has to include this. Shouldn't we always speak with gentleness and respect? But I am sure you have known Christians who disrespect people from other religions or with worldly lifestyles.
- Always keep a clear conscience in your dealings with people in the world.
- There will be people who speak against your good conduct. The goal is that they will be ashamed of their slander because of your loving response.

Can you imagine the impact on our world if every Christian obeyed this word on testifying about Christ?

Christ purchased our salvation through his suffering

[18] For Christ also suffered once for sins, the righteous for the unrighteous, to bring you to God. He was put to death in the body but made alive in the Spirit.

Jesus is the supreme example of suffering for doing good. Even though he lived a perfect life, he died the cruelest death possible; not for his sin, but for your sin and mine. In love, the righteous died for the unrighteous. Sin is the cause of all suffering, Christ's, and ours. Yet even in the case of his beloved Son, it was God's will that he would suffer, to fulfill a greater purpose.

We need that same love for the unrighteous people in this world! And we don't have to die for them; just share the good news of salvation! Thank God, Jesus died for the sin of the whole world once for all, restoring us to fellowship with God and bringing us into his presence. The best way to help those in need around you is to bring them to the Lord, to a new life through salvation in Christ.

Your suffering is not in vain! God can always redeem the situation and glorify himself in it! Unlike Christ's suffering, it is not once and for all; it may be many times, but it doesn't even begin to compare with Christ's suffering on the cross. The same Spirit that brought him back to life will do the same for you after you come through your suffering.

Imprisoned spirits?

[19] After being made alive, he went and made proclamation to the imprisoned spirits— [20] to those who were disobedient long ago when God waited patiently in the days of Noah while the ark was being built. In it only a few people, eight in all, were saved through water, [21] and this water symbolizes baptism that now saves you also.

These are hard verses; the Bible doesn't mention this anywhere else. This is what they say:

- These people were from *"long ago... in the days of Noah."* That probably means that it doesn't apply to people today.
- It was their disobedience which led God to destroy the whole world. Noah was building the ark, but instead of

entering the ark and being saved, they laughed at him. Nonetheless, God patiently waited for them to repent.
- Their spirits were imprisoned. Waiting the final judgment? In some special place? Did they still have the chance to repent? Many times, when the Old Testament uses the word "spirit," it refers to angels or demons. In this case, it would seem to be demons, since they were imprisoned. How did they respond when Christ preached to them?
- They are still important to God, and Christ went in the Spirit and preached to them (during his life here on earth, or during the three days he was in the grave?). It doesn't say how they responded.
- Although it doesn't answer all the questions, Peter's words in his second letter (2 Pet. 2:4-5) may help us understand these "spirits": *For if God did not spare angels when they sinned, but sent them to hell, putting them in chains of darkness to be held for judgment; if he did not spare the ancient world when he brought the flood on its ungodly people, but protected Noah, a preacher of righteousness, and seven others.*

Peter uses Noah's experience to introduce the theme of baptism. Various aspects of the Old Testament serve as types or symbols of New Covenant realities. In this image, Christ would be the ark that saves us. Peter also says that baptism saves us, but this needs to be considered in the context of all biblical teachings on baptism. We know that baptism is the *symbol* of the decision we make to accept Christ as Lord and Savior. Baptism is essential; it is not optional for the believer to be baptized in water as a symbol of the death of old nature and the new birth, but baptism does not save you.

Baptism

Baptism is not the removal of dirt from the body but the pledge of a clear conscience toward God. It saves you by the resurrection of Jesus Christ, [22] who has gone into heaven and is at God's right hand—with angels, authorities and powers in submission to him.

The Bible describes the meaning of baptism in various ways. It is clearly spiritual; it has nothing to do with taking a bath to cleanse the body. It is a covenant we make with God, a commitment, to walk according to God's will and maintain a clear conscience.

From speaking about the current experience of these believers, Peter is moved to exalt Jesus Christ. His victory over death in his resurrection, which Peter witnessed, makes our salvation possible. Jesus then ascended to heaven and sits at the Father's right hand. Every spiritual being (angels, authorities, powers, demons—even the very devil who is attacking these believers) is in submission to God. Thus, the chapter ends with the same word that appears in the first verse: submission. It is that heavenly reality which should be our reality as well. We should submit to every earthly authority, but primarily to God.

Are you submitted to Christ's lordship? Are you practicing the submission to authority that this chapter teaches?

7

A new perspective on suffering
1 Peter 4

This chapter begins with "therefore." When we study the Bible and encounter that word, we must always consider what it is "there for." In this case, it refers to Chapter 3, verse 18 (verses 19-22 are parenthetical). There Peter was talking about Christ, the righteous one, suffering for us, the unrighteous. Christ is our example; walking in fellowship with him gives us a new perspective on suffering. Peter offers us three transformative approaches to suffering.

1: A new attitude

Although these believers had experienced intense persecution, Peter says they need to endure it and even submit to masters (in the case of servants or slaves), husbands (for married women), and every earthly authority—even if they are cruel! When is Peter going to promise an end to the suffering and a happy life ever after? Not now! This is a call to arms, but not with the usual weapons. He calls us to something even more difficult! God's way may not be an easy out, but it is infinitely better:

¹Therefore, since Christ suffered in his body, arm yourselves also with the same attitude, because whoever suffers in the body is done with sin. ² As a result, they do not live the rest of their earthly lives for evil human desires, but rather for the will of God.

Victory in suffering starts with having Christ's mind and thinking like the man of sorrows. This change of attitude affects all of life and challenges our typical attempts to do everything possible to avoid suffering:

- Pills, alcohol, drugs, fleshly pleasures, and endless entertainment (movies, TV, and Internet).
- The pursuit of wealth (or borrowed money) to buy vacations and other goodies.
- Filling life with activity, work, and whatever is necessary to avoid the reality of our problems.

I have heard preachers say that Christ already suffered so that we don't have to suffer. The Bible says that the suffering Savior is our example, and Paul affirms that in Philippians 2:5-11. As Jesus trusted his Father to the extreme of an agonizing crucifixion, God calls us to trust in him and accept the suffering, even to rejoice in it. We "arm" ourselves with this attitude, as a weapon that will enable us to defeat despair and fear. Our attitudes can be as powerful as worldly weapons!

Understand the purpose of suffering

We can take on Christ's attitude because we know that our suffering has a purpose and will result in a positive outcome. In Christ's case, it was our salvation. For us, it is sanctification, becoming more like Jesus. It's a process, and we see how it works in these first two verses:

1. Suffering pushes us to make a break with sin. If you have suffered in your body, you can declare: "I'm done with sin." Unfortunately, the journey to genuine repentance is often marked by illness, imprisonment, or persecution.
2. It is a process and change that will last the rest of your earthly life. The natural thing, which we observe around us all the time, is to satisfy our human desires. We already know what they are, although Peter lists some of them in verse three and the first verse of chapter two.

> We can't serve two masters (God and the flesh); God may allow the suffering necessary to bring us to repentance so we no longer satisfy our fleshly desires.
> 3. Now we long to do God's will: "Not my will, what I want, but your will, Father, what you want." To do his will, you have to know what it is, shape your mind with God's Word, submit every decision to God, and learn to listen to the Holy Spirit to discern his will. Now, the most important thing is to glorify and please God, not yourself. You can force yourself to do God's will, but if you have a bad attitude, it doesn't please him. Christ's attitude is a complete disposition and surrender to God's will. That is your weapon in overcoming sin.

Are you ready to live the rest of your life without *chasing your own desires* (NLT) or *the lusts of men* (NASB), without satisfying your human desires? Can you imagine just doing God's will? Unfortunately, sin can have a firm grip on us, and it may take intense suffering to bring us to the point of renouncing our fleshly desires and longing for God's will. That is true faith, believing that God knows better than we how to live this life to the fullest. The experience of millions of Christians confirms that.

³ For you have spent enough time in the past doing what pagans choose to do—living in debauchery, lust, drunkenness, orgies, carousing and detestable idolatry.

Wasted time

Peter names some of the human passions that we typically satisfy unbelievers and our flesh. We all lived that way in the past, but it's a waste of our time and our lives. Peter knows that some Christians still struggle with them and includes them here. It is time to give them up for good:

- Debauchery (immorality, sensuality); excessive indulgence in sensual pleasures, especially sexual, without self-control or thinking about the consequences.
- Lust: Pornography, sex outside of marriage, homosexuality.
- Drunkenness: Excessive use of alcohol or drugs.
- Orgies: Perverse sexual activity.
- Carousing (wild parties).
- Detestable idolatry: Not limited to the worship of statues, but anything that takes God's place as most important in our lives, especially perverse, abominable things.

Now God calls us to redeem the time and live to please him. We believe in the "depravity" of men and women without Christ. Even though they may not be involved in these sins and may be decent people, without Christ, they are lost.

Paul explains this depravity in Romans 1:29-32:

> *They have become filled with every kind of wickedness, evil, greed and depravity. They are full of envy, murder, strife, deceit and malice. They are gossips, slanderers, God-haters, insolent, arrogant and boastful; they invent ways of doing evil; they disobey their parents; they have no understanding, no fidelity, no love, no mercy. Although they know God's righteous decree that those who do such things deserve death, they not only continue to do these very things but also approve of those who practice them.*

We battle our sinful desires, the pressure of a world that doesn't know Christ, and the devil, as Paul explains in Ephesians 2:1-2:

> As for you, you were dead in your transgressions and sins, in which you used to live when you followed the ways of this world and of the ruler of the kingdom of the air, the spirit who is now at work in those who are disobedient.

This total change will affect our relationships with friends and family.

Old friends in the world

⁴ They are surprised that you do not join them in their reckless, wild living, and they heap abuse on you.

NTV: *Of course, your former friends are surprised when you no longer plunge into the flood of wild and destructive things they do. So they slander you.*

When I was a child, immorality was still frowned on. I have seen an enormous change in today's world. Christian morality is often seen as extreme, rigid, and unreal. Don't we see a flood of wild and reckless living around us every day? Do you know people who can't understand why you disapprove of their immorality? If they insult you, consider it a part of your suffering for Christ. Part of the change in your new life may be distancing yourself from old friends in favor of friends who share Jesus' attitude and the commitment to walk in holiness. You may feel pressured to accept their lifestyle, but remember the following verse:

⁵ But they will have to give account to him who is ready to judge the living and the dead.

There is a coming judgment, with rewards for those who live righteously and eternal punishment for sinners. How will it go for you when you have to give an account to God?

Most people in the world live for the moment and give little thought to what will happen after they die. Knowing about the coming judgment and Christ's soon return, we should do everything we can to prepare ourselves and others.

2: A new vision and hope for the future

⁶ For this is the reason the gospel was preached even to those who are now dead, so that they might be judged according to human standards in regard to the body, but live according to God in regard to the spirit.

This is another difficult verse, perhaps related to what Peter said about Christ preaching to imprisoned spirits (1 Pet. 3:4-5). These people somehow had the opportunity in the spirit to respond to the Gospel, repent, and follow God. They had already been judged by the world's standards for what they had done on earth. They might be believers who suffered under man's judgment and died, but are now alive in the spirit.

Preach the Gospel

Despite the difficulties with this verse, there is important teaching here:

- We have the responsibility to preach the Gospel, to save as many as possible from being condemned to hell.
- The world judges according to human standards, such as appearance, status, and wealth. Christians are often criticized as being narrow-minded and judgmental, but unbelievers can be even more judgmental.
- More important than focusing on God's judgment is to live for God and focus on the Spirit instead of the flesh.
- The believer's experience parallels Christ's: both suffer in the flesh and both die, but, despite the death, both live in the spirit.

Despite the pain, we know that Christ is the answer, and he has something much better prepared for us in the future. It is a privilege and blessing to share that news with everyone, and you will feel Christ's presence and forget about your suffering as you focus on things of eternal significance.

Prepare for the end
⁷ The end of all things is near.

There is an urgency to get our lives in order, as time is running out. Jesus is coming soon, and this world will end. In light of this urgency, we must establish priorities and incorporate various practices into our daily lives. We know that this suffering is temporary, so we focus on preparing the church and ourselves for that glorious day of Christ's return.

1. *Therefore be alert and of sober mind so that you may pray.*

It is easy to get lazy in prayer. Still, in the midst of persecution, suffering, and the pressure to conform to the ways of the world, communion with God is even more important in maintaining a positive focus.

Peter mentions two things that help us in prayer:

- Be alert, clear-minded, and *of sound judgment* (GNB). That's not easy with so many things on the Internet and in the media to contaminate the mind. It's hard to know what is true and what is fake news, making it more critical than ever to be molded by God's Word so we can think clearly. The Greek word can encompass the idea of self-discipline, which is crucial in developing and maintaining a devotional life.
- Be of sober mind. Vocabulary.com defines "sober" as "not drunk, logical or realistic about something, dignified and somber in manner or character, and committed to

keeping promises, quiet and restrained." With all the extremes in today's world and so much talk on the Internet, it is easy to live in fear and lose perspective. Some are afraid of the end of the world, but we have nothing to fear.

2. *[8] Above all, love each other deeply, because love covers over a multitude of sins.*

Jesus said (Jn. 17) that our love should be a witness to the world that the Gospel is true. His new commandment (Jn. 13:30) is to love one another as he has loved us. That is a challenge for us, because Christ's love is intense. Our brothers' and sisters' love helps us endure persecution in the last days. Love doesn't ignore sin, but is more potent than offense and judgment, and ready to forgive any offense. The combination of prayer and love, which leads to repentance and covers a multitude of sins, prepares us for Christ's return. What does loving deeply mean to you? Can you say you are obeying this command?

3. *[9] Offer hospitality to one another without grumbling.*

We don't hear much about this today, but God values hospitality. A natural result of our love should be blessing and helping others with the homes and food God has blessed us with. It is a joy and a privilege to serve others, not thinking about the cost or complaining about the person we're hosting, but trusting God to provide everything necessary to bless them. Opening our homes gives us a good opportunity to love deeply and spoil our guests. What opportunities do you have to practice hospitality? How can you encourage it in your church?

4. *[10] Each of you should use whatever gift you have received to serve others, as faithful stewards of God's grace in its various forms.*

In the face of suffering, pressure from the world to sin, and the uncertainty of the world situation, God calls us to be busy serving in the church. Peter speaks here of a diversity of spiritual gifts, which are for the benefit of the whole church. Every believer receives a gift from God; our part is to use it faithfully. Do you know what your gift is? (Or gifts; you can have more than one.) Are you using it to serve others around you? What does it mean to be a faithful steward? Can you say that you are? If not, what do you need to change?

5. *[11] If anyone speaks, they should do so as one who speaks the very words of God.*

That speaking gift can take the form of teaching, preaching, or prophesying. It is always a sacred responsibility to share a word in Jesus' Name.

6. *If anyone serves, they should do so with the strength God provides.*

Spiritual gifts are supernatural manifestations of the Holy Spirit; any service or ministry should demonstrate God's power. The gift of service is not as impressive as miracles or prophecy, but is equally vital in the church, facilitating its smooth functioning.

Other teachings on spiritual gifts are found in Romans 12, 1 Corinthians 12 and 14, and Ephesians 5.

So that in all things God may be praised through Jesus Christ. To him be the glory and the power forever and ever. Amen.

When we obey this word, God's power is manifest, and he is glorified. The temptation for those who operate in impressive gifts is to seek glory, fame, and power for themselves. Sometimes, after years of ministry, we forget about God's power and minister in the flesh. We must always let God's power flow in our ministry and give him all the glory and praise.

It is possible to complain and despair in your suffering. Preaching the Gospel and being busy with the work of the church gives you a broader vision of what God wants to do today, and of heaven and God's coming kingdom.

3: New joy in the midst of suffering

[12] Dear friends, do not be surprised at the fiery ordeal that has come on you to test you, as though something strange were happening to you.

It's not unusual to be in the fire. Many Christians raised on the teachings of prosperity and constant blessings aren't ready for trials and persecution, but Jesus said they would be part of this life (Jn. 15:20). We may have heard that, but the intensity of the trials still surprises us. Have you ever asked God: "Why? What have I done wrong? Are you angry with me? Am I in sin? Does the fire have to be this hot?"

The good news for these believers is that they are surviving the test. They haven't given up. And you? How are you holding up in the trial? Are you in the fire? This is what Peter says our response should be:

[13] But rejoice inasmuch as you participate in the sufferings of Christ, so that you may be overjoyed when his glory is revealed.

How to rejoice in the middle of the flames

It isn't easy. Only the joy of the Lord and looking beyond the trial to the reward and promise of eternal life can enable you to rejoice. You are participating in the sufferings of Christ! In the fire, we experience an intimacy with Christ we never knew before.

You rarely hear that perspective today, but it was common in the early centuries of the church:

- Acts 5:41: *The apostles left the Sanhedrin, rejoicing because they had been counted worthy of suffering disgrace for the Name.*
- Philippians 3:10: *I want to know Christ—yes, to know the power of his resurrection and participation in his sufferings, becoming like him in his death.*

Our joy as believers is very different than the joy we used to experience in the world. We need to focus on the blessed hope of being with Christ for eternity, and the anticipation of seeing his glory when he returns. Honestly, can you be happy about participating in Christ's sufferings? Have you ever experienced that joy?

14 If you are insulted because of the name of Christ, you are blessed, for the Spirit of glory and of God rests on you.

Once again, this reminds us of the Beatitudes in Matthew 5. Here, a special touch of the Holy Spirit is promised for those who are insulted because of Christ (not because of something foolish you have done).

15 If you suffer, it should not be as a murderer or thief or any other kind of criminal, or even as a meddler. 16 However, if you suffer as a Christian, do not be ashamed, but praise God that you bear that name.

He has repeated it several times in this letter: There is no benefit in suffering because you've committed some crime and are suffering its consequences. To count as suffering for being a Christian, it should be evident to all that we bear his name and reflect his life. Never be ashamed of some insult because you are "different" or a "fanatic." If they insult you because you go to church, carry a Bible, or don't take part in the world's perversions, praise the Lord!

17 For it is time for judgment to begin with God's household; and if it begins with us, what will the outcome be for those who do not obey the gospel of God? 18 And,

"If it is hard for the righteous to be saved,
  what will become of the ungodly and the sinner?"

These verses are frequently quoted, and with good reason. Judgment is real, and can be brutal:

- Everyone will be judged.
- Judgement of Christians had already started in Peter's day and continues right now. God wants to purify his church and prepare a spotless bride for his Son.
- If it is hard for the righteous to be saved, imagine what awaits the ungodly and sinners.

Is it possible you or your church are experiencing God's judgment right now? In his mercy, God is preparing us for judgment day. Those who are in rebellion have good reason to be afraid, because: *It is a dreadful thing to fall into the hands of the living God* (Heb. 10:31; Heb. 10:19-39 is a passage full of good counsel for believers suffering persecution).

The perspective that makes sense of the suffering

19 So then, those who suffer according to God's will should commit themselves to their faithful Creator and continue to do good.

Can it be God's will for you to suffer? That's what Peter says! It should give us comfort remembering that God is sovereign and could save us from the persecution and suffering, but he allows it, because, as we have already seen, he has a purpose in it. No matter how hard it is, the chapter finishes with three simple ways to maintain this new perspective on suffering:

- Keep trusting in your faithful Father.
- Give your life to him.
- Never stop doing good.

8

Counsel for elders, youth, and everyone
1 Peter 5

Peter has addressed suffering as a common experience of believers, and presented submission as the foundation for every relationship: servants (or slaves) and their masters, wives and husbands, the government, and every Christian's attitude toward God's will. Now he turns to church leaders.

For elders

¹To the elders among you, I appeal as a fellow elder and a witness of Christ's sufferings who also will share in the glory to be revealed: ² Be shepherds of God's flock that is under your care, watching over them—not because you must, but because you are willing, as God wants you to be; not pursuing dishonest gain, but eager to serve.

An elder could simply be an older man in the congregation, but here Peter is referring to church leaders. Even though he is one of the principal apostles, he is also an elder. Like other elders, he will share in Christ's glory when Jesus is revealed to the world, but he holds a special place as an eye-witness of Christ's sufferings.

We don't necessarily need to call them elders, but it is essential to follow the New Testament order of church leadership. I am aware of large churches that do not have any elders. The New

Testament gives clear qualifications for them (1 Tim. 3:1-7, Titus 1:5-9). Here is Peter's counsel to the elders:

- They are shepherds (or pastors; it is the same Greek word) of God's flock. They watch over (are overseers) of sheep that belong to God. Jesus identified himself as a pastor, or shepherd (Jn. 10:1-18; Lk. 15:3-7).
- Their task is to care for that flock as a shepherd. There is a crying need today for pastoral care of God's sheep by a pastor who shares his love and counsel and is genuinely concerned for their well-being. Part of shepherding is feeding: It is the elder's responsibility to teach God's Word and provide solid food for his sheep. This is the same commission Peter received the morning he was restored on the beach, as described in John 21. Jesus commanded him to feed, care for, and shepherd his sheep. Peter took that very seriously and obeyed it; now he passes that same commission on to the church elders.
- It is a charge given by God. It's not easy; they are accountable to the chief shepherd. Ezekiel 34:1-10 provides a vivid description of how the shepherds in Israel failed.
- An elder should never serve out of obligation. We should never pressure someone or use guilt to make them serve.
- Anyone seeking the position for financial gain is disqualified. In many cases, the elder is a volunteer, but even in Peter's day, some pastors were getting rich. This doesn't mean that a pastor should not receive a fair salary for his labors (Matt. 10:9-10; 1 Cor. 9:1-18; 1 Tim. 5:17-18).
- The elder should be eager to serve. Jesus said that if you want to be great, you must be everyone's servant (Matt. 20:26-28; Mk. 10:42-45; Lk. 22:26; Jn. 13:12-17).

³ Do not lord it over those entrusted to you, but being examples to the flock.

A heavy hand is never appropriate for church leaders. Pride and self-exaltation will destroy an elder. Peter reflects what he learned from his Master (Mk. 10:42). There is no place in church leadership for someone on a "power trip," or for hypocrites.

Elders lead by example, not by force. For the elder to be an example, the sheep must see him and know him. It can't be through TV or the Internet, or just preaching in the pulpit; the sheep need a good example of a husband and father as well. To become an elder, you should already be known for that good testimony.

⁴ And when the Chief Shepherd appears, you will receive the crown of glory that will never fade away.

There is a reward, but it's not necessarily financial or even in this life. We must serve with the expectation of Christ's return as the Chief Shepherd, the Prince of pastors, the pastor par excellence. He will judge your service, and if it is good, you will receive a crown of glory.

If you are an elder, pastor, or church leader, these verses provide a good opportunity for self-examination. We see that *who you are* is more important than what you *do*. If your relationship to Christ is solid and you have this attitude, God can use you, and ministry will flow. On the other hand, it is possible to be a good preacher and administrator, but if there is a problem here, your ministry will not be successful in God's eyes.

If you want to be an elder or church leader, these are the qualities you should model and develop in your life now. If you are in a position to evaluate someone to be a pastor or elder, look for them in that person.

For young people
⁵In the same way, you who are younger, submit yourselves to your elders.

Peter already commanded servants and wives to submit, now he commands young people, *"in the same way."* In the same way he instructed servants and wives, they are to submit. That is never easy, but it's even harder for a teenager! We can assume that when Peter says "elders" here, that includes not only leaders but anyone older. Where is that honor and respect for elders? This is such a foundational attitude for the Christian life at every level of the church, and it is sorely lacking. It is a great help to elders to have a submissive flock (Heb. 13:17), and that attitude should start in youth. If you are a young person, do you have that attitude toward older people in general, and toward the elders who pastor your church?

Counsel for everyone in the church
All of you, clothe yourselves with humility toward one another, because,

*"God opposes the proud
   but shows favor to the humble."*

As Peter finishes his letter, he addresses every believer. The necessary attitude in every relationship is humility; no one is exempt from the temptation of pride. The proud person is fighting against God, who opposes the proud, and exalts or shows favor to the humble. Here, Peter cites Proverbs 3:34. If it seems like God is against you, could it be that you need to deal with your pride? God freely gives his grace to the humble. Are you experiencing that grace? If not, you may need to humble yourself.

Counsel for elders, youth, and everyone

⁶ Humble yourselves, therefore, under God's mighty hand, that he may lift you up in due time.

God will frustrate every effort to exalt yourself, and he has a mighty hand. Trust in God that he will lift you up at the right time. That's usually later than we would like, but it is much wiser to wait for his time. How do you humble yourself?

- Look for every opportunity to serve.
- Always take the lower place, the last one in line.
- Practice submission. In every situation, look for the person in authority and submit to them.

Christ is our example here (Phil. 2:8-9). The humble person has given up trusting in his own power, wisdom, and righteousness, and instead looks for everything from God. It's much better to take the initiative and humble yourself, but if you don't, God loves you so much that he will often do it for you.

(I have written a book on this subject called <u>Humble Yourself</u>.)

⁷ Cast all your anxiety on him because he cares for you.

There will always be cause for anxiety, especially if you're persecuted and suffering like these believers were, but God will take care of you. You don't have to be anxious; entrust your worries and concerns into God's hands. He knows how to manage them, and will free you from that anxiety. Don't submit to the circumstances, but to God, who controls them.

⁸ Be alert and of sober mind. Your enemy the devil prowls around like a roaring lion looking for someone to devour. ⁹ Resist him, standing firm in the faith, because you know that the family of believers throughout the world is undergoing the same kind of sufferings.

We are in a spiritual war. There is a devil, and he wants to destroy and devour you. He is merciless. He is your enemy; it's not your spouse, your boss, or your pastor (Eph. 6:12). He looks for someone going through trials, sickness, or depression. He waits until you're at your weakest and lowest point, and, like a lion, attacks. You're not unique; believers all over the world are subject to the same temptations and attacks. God will help you, but there are things you must do:

- **Be alert.** There is no chance to rest. The moment you let your guard down, the lion will attack. Watch what is going around you and within you, in your emotions and frustrations.
- **Be sober, wise, and self-controlled.** When you look at perversion on TV or the Internet, you open a door to the devil. When you lack self-control and visit bars or other places full of temptations, you become a target for the devil.
- **Resist him.** When you find yourself face to face with the devil, don't surrender. Resist him. James 4:7 adds a promise: *Resist the devil and he will flee from you.* Claim that promise and stay strong in the fight.
- **Stand firm in the faith.** Your faith is your shield against his attacks (Eph. 6:16). Don't allow doubt to enter your mind. Remind the devil who you are – and who he is.

[10] *And the God of all grace, who called you to his eternal glory in Christ, after you have suffered a little while, will himself restore you and make you strong, firm and steadfast.* [11] *To him be the power for ever and ever. Amen.*

There is no promise of deliverance from suffering. God may allow it. You may even stumble at times. But this is the promise: after a little while, God will restore you and make you strong, firm, and steadfast. God himself has called you, and he calls you with a purpose: To share in his eternal glory in Christ. Surely he will do what is necessary to get you to heaven. He is the God of all grace.

That knowledge leads Peter to praise him: May the power and glory for ever and ever be for Christ.

Final greetings

¹² With the help of Silas, whom I regard as a faithful brother, I have written to you briefly, encouraging you and testifying that this is the true grace of God. Stand fast in it.

Are you suffering? Peter reminds them of a gift: God's grace. If they stand fast in this grace, everything will be alright. Peter's purpose has been to encourage and confirm them in this grace. He knows how easy it is to be unstable, like children, and be up and down in the trials, but if we learn to live by God's grace, we can have stability.

Are there unfaithful brothers? Probably. Silas was a faithful brother. He has been special to Peter, who had little education and probably didn't know how to write Greek. Silas helped him. This is the same brother whom Paul took with him on his second missionary journey, and was his cellmate in Philippi. He was a prophet (Acts 15:32) and carried the decision of the Jerusalem council to Antioch. Although it sometimes seems like Peter and Paul were in different worlds, there was a fellowship between them, and possibly they were both in Rome.

¹³ She who is in Babylon, chosen together with you, sends you her greetings, and so does my son Mark. ¹⁴ Greet one another with a kiss of love.

Babylon is almost certainly Rome; Peter wrote from that city. We are not aware of Peter having any natural children. Mark was a spiritual son, the one who wrote the Gospel based on what Peter told him. He was a cousin of Barnabas and Paul's companion in his Roman imprisonment.

Peace to all of you who are in Christ.

Amid the struggle and persecution, Peter blesses them with the peace of Christ, because they are *in* Christ, a safe and peaceful place. The best place to be!

2 Peter

Three years later (approximately AD 67) Peter wrote this letter to all the churches. The vicious persecution under Nero continued, and Peter realized that his time was short. Interestingly, this was the last book admitted to the New Testament canon. There were doubts about who wrote it, even though Peter identifies himself as the author. He wrote it as an antidote to stagnation and myopia in the Christian life, a problem that continues to plague the church today. They had survived the persecution, but now there was a potent new threat: False prophets, or false teachers. Satan uses various strategies to destroy the church. With its perspective of Christ's imminent return, this letter has an important message for us.

9

How to never fall
2 Peter 1:1-11

¹ Simon Peter, a servant and apostle of Jesus Christ,

To those who through the righteousness of our God and Savior Jesus Christ have received a faith as precious as ours:

A servant
Peter was a key leader in the early church, but, following the teaching and example of his Master, he considers himself a servant. He was also an apostle, but in the kingdom of God the one who wants to be great must be the servant of all. Peter distinguishes himself from the false teachers who were moving in to dominate the churches when he calls himself a servant. Do you know any modern-day "apostles" in the church? Do they have the heart and attitude of a servant?

We all receive grace and faith
Peter also identifies with the people to whom this letter is addressed. Every believer has received the same precious faith. As opposed to the false teachers and Gnostics who claimed special knowledge, Peter says that we all have received the same grace from the Lord. Sometimes we think of faith as something we have to produce; Peter says we *receive* this faith. God gives us the capacity to believe. Jesus' righteousness enables us to be saved; mine is like filthy rags.

Jesus is God

One heresy that has plagued the church through the centuries is the teaching that Jesus is not God. Christ is the stumbling block for several groups, who claim that we worship two (or three) gods. They say the Bible never affirms that Jesus is God, but here Peter clearly states that Jesus Christ is God and Savior.

The fruit of our knowledge of Christ

² Grace and peace be yours in abundance through the knowledge of God and of Jesus our Lord.

Do you want more grace and peace in your life? They come through your knowledge of God. Draw close to Jesus and read the Bible to grow in that knowledge and your experience of his grace and peace. Twice, Peter uses the word "abundance" in this chapter. We shouldn't just *taste* the grace and peace; they should *abound* in us. Are you growing in your knowledge of Jesus? Not just intellectually or in Bible knowledge, but personal knowledge in relationship to him.

Once again, Peter is fighting against the confusion caused by the Gnostic teaching that there is something we must do to receive special knowledge. Peter says grace and peace are the fruits of a personal knowledge of Jesus and our relationship with him.

Everything you need for a godly life

³ His divine power has given us everything we need for a godly life through our knowledge of him who called us by his own glory and goodness. ⁴ Through these he has given us his very great and precious promises, so that through them you may participate in the divine nature, having escaped the corruption in the world caused by evil desires.

Peter emphasizes it: God has already given us everything we need! There is nothing more that the false teachers can offer than what they already have. The same danger exists today when someone offers you a new revelation. Be very careful of what you receive.

The process of your salvation

There is an undeniable progression or process here. You begin lost, destined for hell, and you finish sharing in the divine nature. God acts with his divine power, but you must know him, claim his promises, and fight evil desires.

God calls you.

His glory and goodness motivate him and prompt him to action, as he wants you to share in these blessings.

His divine power makes your redemption and salvation possible.

Once saved, you have to change; you're no longer in charge, God is. But he has done everything necessary to make that change possible, giving you everything that you need for a godly life.

You receive these through the knowledge God gives you of himself.

Knowing something of his holiness and glory, and already having everything you need to obey him, you escape from the corruption in the world caused by evil desires.

God gives you his great and precious promises.

You come to participate in the divine nature.

Most of this process is God's work. Even the knowledge you have of God is a gift, through revelation and the Holy Spirit's work in you. That revelation and knowledge motivate you to flee from sin. Be careful of any teaching that downplays the seriousness of sin and doesn't lead to holiness; you should receive, listen to, and meditate on what has already been revealed.

God's promises

God gives you his promises, but only after going through this process. They are great and precious, and he is not going to give them to someone with a corrupt mind who is all about satisfying the desires of his flesh. It's not possible to count all the promises of the Bible, but there are around 3000. God gives them to us, but we must seek them out and study them. There are "promise boxes" with a card and a promise for every day.

Participate in the divine nature?

How is it possible to participate in God's nature? Does it mean we become gods? Of course not. But with the knowledge God has given you, you experience the miraculous fulfillment of his promises and are freed from sin, and you have a new nature that is closer to the divine than the carnal. If you don't escape the corruption of the world, you can't participate in the divine nature. As Peter commanded us in his first letter (1:16): *Be holy, because I am holy*. We share in his holiness.

Where are you in this process?
Are you growing in your knowledge of God? Have you escaped the corruption in the world? Or do you still live to satisfy the evil desires of your flesh? How many of God's promises do you know? It would be good to have a notebook to write down every promise you find in the Bile, and how and when God fulfills it.

Perhaps the first promise to hold on to is the reality that God has already given you everything you need to live as he commands. Do you believe it? God has done an amazing work for you, and precisely because the goal is something so amazing (to share in the divine nature), you have to make every effort to become like him.

5 For this very reason, make every effort to add to your faith goodness; and to goodness, knowledge; 6 and to knowledge, self-control; and to self-control, perseverance; and to perseverance, godliness; 7 and to godliness, mutual affection; and to mutual affection, love.

Another process!
Some have suggested that these are merely various aspects of the Christian life, without any particular order; however, it's stated here that it's a clear progression, as it's impossible to work on all of these at the same time. It's similar to the progression Paul gives in Romans 5:3-4: *Not only so, but we also glory in our sufferings, because we know that suffering produces perseverance; perseverance, character; and character, hope.*

Here, the foundation is your faith; everything starts with that faith in God:

Faith (true faith always manifests in obedience and action)

Goodness (good conduct, moral excellence)

Knowledge (understanding)

Self-control (many false teachers lack that)

Perseverance (patience)

Godliness (devotion and submission to God)

Mutual (brotherly) affection

Love (agape)

Some observations about this process:

- Everything starts with faith. Without faith in God, you can work and try to be better, but it will all be in the flesh, and you will end up frustrated.
- This probably is not something you master once and for all. For example, self-control could be a lifelong struggle.
- Your knowledge grows with the study of the Word and solid teaching and preaching in the church.
- As many biblical texts affirm, love is the ultimate; it is the goal of your discipleship. It seems hard to have that love without the foundation of the other things.
- Yes, this is hard work. You have to dedicate yourself to this process. But most of these things are also fruits of the Holy Spirit, so as you grow in your communion with the Spirit, he produces them in you.

Can you say you have made every effort to work on these things? Many people make an effort to grow from time to time, going to a seminar or retreat, or reading a book. But for most, it's not a priority. Where are you in this process? What grade (A to F) would you give yourself for each characteristic?

[8] For if you possess these qualities in increasing measure, they will keep you from being ineffective and unproductive in your knowledge of our Lord Jesus Christ. [9] But whoever does not have them is nearsighted and blind, forgetting that they have been cleansed from their past sins.

[10] Therefore, my brothers and sisters, make every effort to confirm your calling and election. For if you do these things, you will never stumble, [11] and you will receive a rich welcome into the eternal kingdom of our Lord and Savior Jesus Christ.

If you do these things, you will never stumble

It is true that works do not save us, but that can make us think that Christ has to do everything, and we don't do anything: "I'm chosen and have my ticket to heaven. Since I can't lose my salvation, I can live as I want to." Peter has encountered this attitude and knows how perilous it can be. If you need more motivation to strengthen yourself and work on these things, Peter gives us various fruits of this work, and the consequences of ignoring it:

- It will cause you to grow in your knowledge of Jesus. Is knowing Jesus better important to you? It doesn't matter if you have been walking with the Lord for twenty years; there is always room for growth in that relationship.
- It will keep you from being ineffective and unproductive. In other words, you will be useful in God's kingdom and productive in your service for him. If you have felt useless, it could be that these things are not evident in your life.
- God chose you and called you, but you have to confirm that call. Are there times when you doubt if you are one of the elect, called by God to follow Jesus? Get to work on these things, and God will confirm that call.
- It will open the doors of Jesus' eternal kingdom to you. Could that mean that if you don't diligently work on these things, the doors won't open for you? I certainly don't want to risk that.
- You will never stumble or fall! That is one of his precious promises, a guarantee: It is not inevitable that you are going to stumble or fall.

Talk about God's promises! That one is tremendous! It is possible never to stumble! These qualities should *abound* in you. Peter has strong words for the person who ignores them:

- He is nearsighted and blind, unable to see what walking with Christ is about.
- He has forgotten that he has been cleansed from his past sins.

Eleven short verses, but what an introduction to this letter! Meditate on this process and consider what God wants for you at this moment. They are so important that Peter says he always has to remind believers of them.

10

Peter's experience
2 Peter 1:12-21

¹² So I will always remind you of these things, even though you know them and are firmly established in the truth you now have.

They may seem very basic, but are so important that it is always good to be reminded of them. Peter knows they have already heard them, and are firmly established in them, but the things he has just written about are salvation issues:

- 1:3: *everything we need for a godly life.* If you don't live a godly life, and don't know what it takes to do so, how can you expect to enter his kingdom?
- 1:8: *if you possess these qualities in increasing measure, they will keep you from being ineffective and unproductive.* John 15 tells us that God cuts off unfruitful branches and burns them.
- 1:10: *make every effort to confirm your calling and election.* There are things you must do to confirm your election.

No wonder Peter wants to remind them! I have heard complaints about a sermon on the basics, but don't be proud! It is good to be reminded of them. How many people are firmly established in them?

The temporary tent of the body
¹³ I think it is right to refresh your memory as long as I live in the tent of this body, ¹⁴ because I know that I will soon put it aside, as

our Lord Jesus Christ has made clear to me. ^{15} And I will make every effort to see that after my departure you will always be able to remember these things.

Like Jesus in the Upper Room the night of his arrest, this weighs on Peter's heart as he nears death.

The youthful Peter we know from the Gospels probably thought very little about death. Young people don't, but as the years progress, death and eternity become increasingly real. Paul referred to the body as a *"clay jar"* (2 Cor. 4:7); Peter calls it a tent. Someday, we will all have to *"put it aside."* By God's grace, it usually serves us well on this earth, but he has a glorified, perfect body waiting for us in heaven.

Making every effort

The person nearing death also wants to leave his survivors equipped to thrive, and Peter feels that he can rest, having done his part by sharing what is most important. Can you say that hard work and diligence characterize your service for the Lord? Do you do everything possible to help your fellow Christians?

The last will and testament of a father (or someone significant in your life) carries special weight. Peter has fulfilled Jesus' command to pastor and feed his sheep (Jn. 21:15-16). We believe that Mark wrote the second gospel, working closely with Peter to record Jesus' words for us.

Before his death…

Many of us don't want to think about death, but are you ready? Do you have everything in order? Does your spouse know what to do if you die? Is there some commitment you need to fulfill? Something you should change so you have no regrets on your deathbed? What kind of legacy are you going to leave?

Peter's own experience

¹⁶ For we did not follow cleverly devised stories when we told you about the coming of our Lord Jesus Christ in power, but we were eyewitnesses of his majesty. ¹⁷ He received honor and glory from God the Father when the voice came to him from the Majestic Glory, saying, "This is my Son, whom I love; with him I am well pleased." ¹⁸ We ourselves heard this voice that came from heaven when we were with him on the sacred mountain.

Of all the apostles, Peter probably had the most personal experience with Jesus. The Gospels certainly say more about him than any other disciple. He spent many hours with Jesus, touched him, and walked on the water toward him. Of those three years walking with Jesus, the most impressive thing for Peter was the Transfiguration (Matt. 17:1-8, Lk. 9:28-36), when he saw Jesus in his glory and heard the voice of the Father affirming his Son.

Jesus is not a myth, and the Gospels are not legends; Peter was there, unlike the false teachers whom he will condemn.

Prophecy inspired by the Spirit

¹⁹ We also have the prophetic message as something completely reliable, and you will do well to pay attention to it, as to a light shining in a dark place, until the day dawns and the morning star rises in your hearts. ²⁰ Above all, you must understand that no prophecy of Scripture came about by the prophet's own interpretation of things. ²¹ For prophecy never had its origin in the human will, but prophets, though human, spoke from God as they were carried along by the Holy Spirit.

It is not just personal experience: our faith is founded on the records of four writers about the life and words of Jesus Christ, and confirmed by Old Testament prophecies fulfilled in Jesus.

- The transfiguration affirmed the truth of the Old Testament, as Moses and Elijah appeared.
- We should pay attention to the prophets.
- Their word is a light shining in dark places.
- Scholars speak of Isaiah's "style" and how Jeremiah "wrote" Lamentations. But those prophets were "carried along" by the Holy Spirit and spoke on behalf of God himself.
- Prophecy never had its origin in the personal understanding of the prophet or from human initiative.

What a beautiful image! The morning star rising in our hearts! That will happen when the Day of the Lord dawns and Jesus returns to this world.

I am the Root and the Offspring of David, and the bright Morning Star.

Revelation 22:16

11

False teachers and their destruction
2 Peter 2

Chapter divisions were added to the Bible much later, and often interrupt the flow of the author's thoughts. This chapter begins with a "but," which means there is a direct connection with the previous chapter. Peter concluded with a strong affirmation of the inspiration and importance of prophecy, but his primary concern is the proliferation of heresy, false doctrine, and false prophets. He took Jesus' words seriously: *For false messiahs and false prophets will appear and perform signs and wonders to deceive, if possible, even the elect. So be on your guard; I have told you everything ahead of time* (Mk. 13:22-23).

Prophecy and false doctrine in today's church

Today's church is sadly lacking in knowledge of the Bible, sound doctrine, church history, and heresies that have affected the church through the centuries. We are very vulnerable to false doctrine! Some people believe that doctrine and theology, and studying them, are not necessary, but for God there is truth and there are lies. Satan is the father of lies and is a deceiver; today, more than ever, he knows that his time is short and is busy deceiving the church.

Paul spoke of the importance of prophecy in 1 Corinthians 14, and warned us in 1 Thessalonians 5:20: *Do not despise prophecy*. However, today it is a controversial topic, and we face the same situation Peter did: there are many false prophets, necessitating caution and discernment. Just as in the Old Testament, there probably are more false than true prophets, but we don't reject the true word from God because of them.

Characteristics of false prophets

¹But there were also false prophets among the people, just as there will be false teachers among you. They will secretly introduce destructive heresies, even denying the sovereign Lord who bought them—bringing swift destruction on themselves. ² Many will follow their depraved conduct and will bring the way of truth into disrepute. ³ In their greed these teachers will exploit you with fabricated stories. Their condemnation has long been hanging over them, and their destruction has not been sleeping.

Do you know how to identify and respond to false prophets and teachers? Many Old Testament Jews accepted them because they said what they wanted to hear, and they persecuted the true prophets of God because they often had a hard word. Here we learn some characteristics of false teachers:

- They secretly introduce destructive heresies.
    - Heresy is always destructive to believers' faith, the purity of biblical teaching, and the spread of the Gospel.
    - He says the false teachers "introduce" the heresies; these are new teachings that were previously unknown.
    - You probably wouldn't think they were coming from the devil; they come secretly, as wolves in sheep's clothing. They may seem to have God's anointing and know all the right words.
- They deny the Lord who bought them (literally, "redeemed" them). They had knowledge of the Gospel, but go to the extreme of denying Jesus.

False teachers and their destruction

- Many will follow their depraved conduct. Prepare to see it accepted in the media and be pressured by "many" to follow the same heresy. It is not just false *doctrine*, but also false *conduct*. Sexual immorality is the most common perversion, since the Greek word is "sensuality," but it probably covers all depraved conduct.
- Because of them, Christianity will be slandered and looked down on.
- They focus on money; they are driven by greed and make up stories to exploit believers and rob them. The NLT says: *In their greed they will make up clever lies to get hold of your money.*

Peter speaks of their "*swift destruction*," with a condemnation that has been hanging over them, which leads into the following verses. As with many aspects of the Christian life that are supposed to occur "swiftly," it can seem to us that they are not happening quickly enough; the delay can be very troubling.

Three examples of the certainty of judgment

Peter now gives three examples from the past to support his confidence that God will judge them. No one is exempt from God's righteous judgment.

- **The angels:** *⁴ For if God did not spare angels when they sinned, but sent them to hell, putting them in chains of darkness to be held for judgment.* They are Satan and a third of the angels who rebelled with him. In this case, there is no chance for repentance or forgiveness. Peter includes these curious things:
    - God sent them to hell.
    - He put them in chains (pits) of darkness.
    - He held them for judgment.

    That raises some questions for us:

- If they are already in hell, chained up, how can they attack us now? The Bible doesn't explain it, but apparently, some are bound up while others are free to oppress us.
- What will happen to them at that judgment? All those angels (including Satan) will be eternally condemned to hell.

- **The ancient world before the flood:** *⁵ If he did not spare the ancient world when he brought the flood on its ungodly people, but protected Noah, a preacher of righteousness, and seven others.* No one else sought God to repent and ask forgiveness, and it was only Noah's righteousness that allowed his family to survive. This is the only time in Scripture that Noah is called a "preacher of righteousness." In the same way Noah resisted the pressure of the ungodly and faithfully preached God's righteousness, these suffering believers can resist the false teachers and persevere in the persecution. God will protect us also.

- **Sodom and Gomorrah:** *⁶ If he condemned the cities of Sodom and Gomorrah by burning them to ashes, and made them an example of what is going to happen to the ungodly.* The first example is of heavenly beings, the second of the destruction of the entire world, and now, judgment focused on two cities known for their perversion. There is no doubt that God will punish the ungodly.

God rescues the righteous

Peter gives a very positive picture of Lot, unlike the story in Genesis 18 and 19, where it seems it was more Abraham's

False teachers and their destruction

intercession than Lot's righteousness which saved him: ⁷ and if he rescued Lot, a righteous man, who was distressed by the depraved conduct of the lawless ⁸ (for that righteous man, living among them day after day, was tormented in his righteous soul by the lawless deeds he saw and heard).

- Lot was distressed by the sin that surrounded him.
- The inhabitants of those cities were depraved, living a lawless life.
- Despite their sin, Lot lived among them and was righteous.
- He saw and heard their lawless deeds.
- Day after day he was tormented in his soul.

Lot wasn't perfect, but God still rescued him, and these readers can be confident that God will rescue them.

⁹ if this is so, then the Lord knows how to rescue the godly from trials and to hold the unrighteous for punishment on the day of judgment. ¹⁰ This is especially true of those who follow the corrupt desire of the flesh and despise authority.

Sin is sin, but some sins are more grievous to the Lord. Here, Peter mentions two:

- Following the corrupt desire of the flesh, *their own twisted sexual desire* (NLT). In this case, it was even worse because they were corrupting the church. Paul said (1 Cor. 3:17) that God will destroy the person who destroys his temple, which is the church.
- Despising authority. In marked contrast to the submission that Peter presented as a foundation of the Christian life in his first letter, these are rebels who despise all authority.

There are two groups, and the examples Peter gave from the Old Testament confirm how God acts:

- The unrighteous, who will be punished on judgment day.
- The godly, who obey God. The Lord knows how to rescue them from trials. That would be good news for these believers who have suffered years of Nero's persecution and now struggle with the deception of false teachers, but they could easily think: How long?

The Bible mentions other sins that are very serious, like causing a little one to stumble (Matt. 18:6). In his description of sin in Romans 1, Paul portrays sexual sin, and especially homosexuality, as the most perverse expression of our fallen, rebellious nature.

The perversion of the false teachers

Peter begins a series of denunciations against the false teachers, using every image he can think of to highlight their perversity.

[10]They are bold and arrogant!

Completely lacking in humility, proud, daring, and self-willed. Watch out for arrogance in church leaders; it is a strong temptation, but it is opposed to the humility Christ demands of his servants. The strong-willed person might say they are just uncompromising in their stand for truth, and that may be, but often it is an expression of pride. The arrogant person almost always lacks submission to the authority of God, the Bible, and others.

They are not afraid to heap abuse on celestial beings; [11] yet even angels, although they are stronger and more powerful, do not heap abuse on such beings when bringing judgment on them from the Lord.

Part of their problem was a lack of respect for celestial beings (literally: *angelic majesties*, probably fallen angels), reviling and scoffing at them, something Peter sees as abominable. We should be careful of how we talk about the devil and his demons. To speak that way in the Lord's presence invites judgment.

¹² But these people blaspheme in matters they do not understand.

He is probably not talking about blasphemy of the Holy Spirit, which is the unpardonable sin. I have observed many preachers or teachers mocking or criticizing other churches or controversial doctrines such as the rapture, the millennium, and spiritual gifts (like speaking in tongues). If someone is in error, we must inform the church about them, but always in humility and never mocking other ministries.

They are like unreasoning animals, creatures of instinct, born only to be caught and destroyed, and like animals they too will perish.
¹³ They will be paid back with harm for the harm they have done.

We reap what we sow. If you have harmed, you will be paid back with harm at some point. Peter is not putting down animals, but he does want to insult the false teachers by equating them to animals. An animal doesn't reason, but lives by his instincts.

Their idea of pleasure is to carouse in broad daylight. They are blots and blemishes, reveling in their pleasures while they feast with you.

Just like the people of Sodom and Gomorrah, they carouse and live by their passions. They have the audacity to carouse and satisfy those passions in broad daylight, totally lacking modesty or shame. Pleasure is their god, even as they join believers in their meals, including the Lord's Supper.

Each one of these faults will be obvious to the person who carefully analyzes and observes them. Don't be deceived by appearances and promises.

14 With eyes full of adultery, they never stop sinning; they seduce the unstable; they are experts in greed—an accursed brood!

Peter heaps up the accusations:

- Their eyes are full of adultery
- They never stop sinning
- They target the unstable and seduce them
- They are experts in greed
- They are accursed

15 They have left the straight way and wandered off to follow the way of Balaam son of Bezer, who loved the wages of wickedness. 16 But he was rebuked for his wrongdoing by a donkey—an animal without speech—who spoke with a human voice and restrained the prophet's madness.

Peter compares them here to the famous prophet Balaam (read his story in Numbers 22-24). At first, he said he couldn't curse Israel, but could only proclaim the word God gave him. But then King Balak paid him, and he cursed Israel. He has forever been an example of someone who perverted serving God.

With the focus on Balaam, it would be easy to overlook something important here: These false teachers and prophets started on the straight way, knowing the Lord, but left it and "wandered off" into error. The departure into error may not be a sudden decision, but rather a gradual process that begins with small steps and ultimately leads to error. Usually, it is money and sensual pleasures that seduce them.

False teachers and their destruction

¹⁷ These people are springs without water and mists driven by a storm (NLT: *as useless as dried-up springs or as mist blown away by the wind*). *Blackest darkness is reserved for them.*

- Springs without water. Everything is about appearances. They promise something refreshing, and their word sounds good, but it's all empty. They never fulfill what they promise.
- Storm-driven mists. Fog that you see but doesn't produce rain; it just makes travel dangerous. They are unstable and untrustworthy.
- Blackest darkness is reserved for them. Like a dense fog, they will receive a strong condemnation.

¹⁸ For they mouth empty, boastful words and, by appealing to the lustful desires of the flesh, they entice people who are just escaping from those who live in error.

- Their words are empty and boastful: *They brag about themselves with empty, foolish boasting* (NLT). There is little of God's Word and much about themselves. At the end of the message, what at first seemed impressive often leaves you wondering: "What exactly did he want to say, and what does it have to do with my life in Christ?"
- They appeal to the lustful desires of the flesh. Perhaps not directly, but they make sexual insinuations and speak more graphically than necessary about sexual sin, often sending your thoughts somewhere they shouldn't go.
- Their target is new believers who have little biblical knowledge and are just escaping from error or sin.

¹⁹ They promise them freedom, while they themselves are slaves of depravity—for "people are slaves to whatever has mastered them."

Are you a slave? Peter repeats what Jesus said (*"Very truly I tell you, everyone who sins is a slave to sin,"* Jn. 8:34). Paul echoed it: *Don't you know that when you offer yourselves to someone as obedient slaves, you are slaves of the one you obey—whether you are slaves to sin, which leads to death, or to obedience, which leads to righteousness?* (Rom. 6:16). You are a slave to whatever has mastered you. What would you honestly say controls you?

Many believe that Christians lack freedom, and promise you freedom to live as you want to, but in reality, they are slaves of depravity. You are a slave of whatever controls you.

Better to never know the Lord

[20] *If they have escaped the corruption of the world by knowing our Lord and Savior Jesus Christ and are again entangled in it and are overcome, they are worse off at the end than they were at the beginning.* [21] *It would have been better for them not to have known the way of righteousness, than to have known it and then to turn their backs on the sacred command that was passed on to them.* [22] *Of them the proverbs are true: "A dog returns to its vomit," and, "A sow that is washed returns to her wallowing in the mud."*

Here it is clear: They knew Jesus. They knew the way of righteousness and the Word of God. They had escaped from the corruption of the world, but were seduced by its pleasures. It often begins with something small, but it is easy to get entangled in sin and suddenly find yourself overcome. At some point, a decision was made to turn their backs on what they knew. In the case of false teachers, they often remain in the church, possibly in a highly visible ministry, and may be known as prophets. But they are overcome by the enemy and by their own sin, and are some of Satan's most effective ministers.

Peter makes an alarming declaration: It is better never to know Christ and the way of righteousness than to know it and leave it. You may know some backslidden believers who confirm how true that is. Hebrews 6:4-8 says something similar:

It is impossible for those who have once been enlightened, who have tasted the heavenly gift, who have shared in the Holy Spirit, who have tasted the goodness of the word of God and the powers of the coming age and who have fallen away, to be brought back to repentance. To their loss they are crucifying the Son of God all over again and subjecting him to public disgrace. Land that drinks in the rain often falling on it and that produces a crop useful to those for whom it is farmed receives the blessing of God. But land that produces thorns and thistles is worthless and is in danger of being cursed. In the end, it will be burned.

For another account of the struggle with false teachers and false apostles, read 2 Corinthians. Today, the danger of false prophets and teachers in the church is more real than ever.

12

Christ is coming soon
2 Peter 3

¹Dear friends, this is now my second letter to you. I have written both of them as reminders to stimulate you to wholesome thinking. ² I want you to recall the words spoken in the past by the holy prophets and the command given by our Lord and Savior through your apostles.

The letter's purpose

In the Greek, this chapter simply starts, "Beloved," but apparently that is too strong for most English translators, who choose to say, "Dear friends." Love is the mark of the believer, and Peter's heart is full of love. He has shared what was weighing on his heart, and now pauses to review the most important points he wants to leave with them. His purpose in the two letters is to refresh their memories. He claims no new revelation. Indeed, Peter says we already have all the revelation we need. There are three important things he has wanted to accomplish in writing them:

- **Remind them** (we are quick to forget!). They had been taught sound doctrine; Peter wants them to be reminded of it so they can refute the false teachers.
- **Stimulate them to wholesome thinking:** *stir up your sincere mind* (NASB) or *arouse pure thoughts in your mind* (GNB). To confront all the false doctrines, they need to think clearly, not be enticed by sensuality or deceived by emotionalism.

- **Draw attention to the words of Scripture.** When there is heresy and false doctrine, the most important thing we can do is return to the Bible, study it, and evaluate new teachings in the light of Scripture.

Peter equates the words of the Old Testament prophets with those of Jesus, as recorded by the apostles. The New Testament was already in its initial stages of formation. The Old Testament prophets not only wrote for Israel, they also have much to teach us today. Have you read, studied, and meditated on those prophets?

What command given by Jesus is he referring to? It could be the new command to love each other as he has loved us, or simply the whole Christian gospel.

Peter has discussed his past and the current challenges facing the church; now he will address what to expect in the future.

Scoffers in the last days

³ Above all, you must understand that in the last days scoffers will come, scoffing and following their own evil desires. ⁴ They will say, "Where is this 'coming' he promised? Ever since our ancestors died, everything goes on as it has since the beginning of creation."

Peter wants them to prepare for the last days. If these first-century Christians were already in the last days, imagine us! There are people, even in church, who are tired of hearing about Christ's return. They are cynics; nothing has changed despite all the "prophecies" that Christ would come on a specific date.

- Scoffers will come. Have you known some?

- They follow their evil desires and often misinterpret the Bible or point to some teaching that avoids talking about crucifying the flesh and allows much "freedom" to sin.
- They will mock and make fun of those who believe the Bible and its promises.

Our belief in the return of Christ is not an optional doctrine. It is the foundation of our hope and is a clear New Testament promise. We must live in the light of his soon return.

^{5}But they deliberately forget that long ago by God's word the heavens came into being and the earth was formed out of water and by water. ^{6}By these waters also the world of that time was deluged and destroyed. ^{7}By the same word the present heavens and earth are reserved for fire, being kept for the day of judgment and destruction of the ungodly.

Never forget the power of God's word:

- Heaven and earth were created by his word.
- Flood waters were released to destroy the earth in the days of Noah.
- That same word will declare the destruction of the heavens and the earth.

False teachers "deliberately" ignore or question what God's word has accomplished, but they will be judged. The first judgment was by water; the coming judgment will be by fire.

We need to be careful with how we interpret the "*destruction of the ungodly.*" Be cautious of forming doctrines from isolated verses. There is a popular teaching called "annihilationism," which says that the devil, his demons, and all those who have never accepted Christ will simply be destroyed. They may cite verse 7 to support it, but many Scriptures speak of the eternal punishment of sinners.

The reminder of God's power - in creation, the judgment of the ancient world in the flood, and the coming judgment - should move these believers to sound thinking and reverence for God and the truth.

God wants everyone to come to repentance

⁸ But do not forget this one thing, dear friends: With the Lord a day is like a thousand years, and a thousand years are like a day. ⁹ The Lord is not slow in keeping his promise, as some understand slowness. Instead, he is patient with you, not wanting anyone to perish, but everyone to come to repentance.

In our struggle with doubt and false teachers regarding Christ's return, there are three essential things to remember:

- God operates outside our understanding of time. What seems like forever to us (for example, a thousand years) is nothing to the Lord (twenty-four hours).
- Who are we to say that God is slow in keeping his promise?
- He is simply being patient with us.

Although we need to form doctrines based on all of Scripture, Peter makes two explicit declarations about God's will:

- Negatively, God doesn't want anyone to perish.
- Positively, he wants everyone to come to repentance.

When we evangelize, we are working with God to bring as many as possible to repentance. God never wants to send anyone to hell. The only reason he delays sending Christ back to this earth is to allow more to be saved.

The day of the Lord
¹⁰ But the day of the Lord will come like a thief. The heavens will disappear with a roar; the elements will be destroyed by fire, and the earth and everything done in it will be laid bare.

It is not just a renewal of this earth, with a kingdom established in what is now Israel. All the animals, plants, and everything else we know on this earth will be burned, not in a process lasting months or years, but disappearing with a great roar. That often evokes images of a nuclear explosion or some other natural phenomenon, but be cautious of speculating about such significant matters. It is alarming to think about this destruction, but your future is safe in God's hands.

What we do know is that Christ will come like a thief, unexpectedly. Be cautious of those who claim to know the date of his coming. As Jesus said: *"You also must be ready, because the Son of Man will come at an hour when you do not expect him"* (Lk. 12:40).

How to live in the light of his coming
¹¹ Since everything will be destroyed in this way, what kind of people ought you to be? You ought to live holy and godly lives ¹² as you look forward to the day of God and speed its coming. That day will bring about the destruction of the heavens by fire, and the elements will melt in the heat. ¹³ But in keeping with his promise we are looking forward to a new heaven and a new earth, where righteousness dwells. ¹⁴ So then, dear friends, since you are looking forward to this, make every effort to be found spotless, blameless and at peace with him.

There is no need to fear, but rather:

- Wait expectantly for the coming of that day while keeping this truth in mind.

- Look forward to the new heavens and earth, which will be much better than what we know now.
- Anticipate righteousness dwelling on that new earth.
- Look forward to the day and speed its coming by doing everything possible to prepare the Body of Christ and by encouraging missions and evangelism. Amazingly, we have a part to play in when that day comes!

Is this critical event front and center in your thoughts? Or is it just a nice idea you think about once in a while, since you are caught up with life in this world? Are you involved in anything that would speed its coming?

In light of this, we should have fear and reverence for God:

- Living holy and godly lives.
- Making every effort to be found spotless.
- Doing our best to be faultless and blameless.
- Being diligent to maintain our peace with God.

These things, and not conjecture about details of Christ's coming and the future, should fill our minds and our time. How are you doing with them?

Paul

¹⁵ Bear in mind that our Lord's patience means salvation, just as our dear brother Paul also wrote you with the wisdom that God gave him. ¹⁶ He writes the same way in all his letters, speaking in them of these matters. His letters contain some things that are hard to understand, which ignorant and unstable people distort, as they do the other Scriptures, to their own destruction.

This is a fascinating reference to Paul. Peter respects him and recognizes his God-given wisdom. Even though it doesn't seem like a natural chemistry existed between Peter and Paul, the two did agree on the importance of Christ's return and the need for a holy life. At the same time, Peter recognizes that it is hard to understand some things that Paul wrote, which enabled the false teachers to pervert his teachings.

In what is truly impressive so early in the church's history, Peter refers to Paul's letters and *"the other Scriptures,"* granting his letters the same status as the Old Testament.

Final counsel

^{17} Therefore, dear friends, since you have been forewarned, be on your guard so that you may not be carried away by the error of the lawless and fall from your secure position. ^{18} But grow in the grace and knowledge of our Lord and Savior Jesus Christ. To him be glory both now and forever! Amen.

These brothers can't plead ignorance. They have been given this teaching, and now they are responsible for their obedience to it. There are several things that you need to do:

- Be on your guard.
- If you are not alert, you could easily get carried away by the error of the *"lawless,"* unprincipled, false teachers.
- If that happens, you could fall from your secure position.
- On the positive side, you need to grow in the grace and knowledge of Jesus Christ.

www.ingramcontent.com/pod-product-compliance
Lightning Source LLC
Chambersburg PA
CBHW071301040426
42444CB00009B/1818